THE NEW
GREENHOUSE GARDENING
FOR EVERYONE

By Ernest Chabot

Gramercy Publishing Company·New York

Contents

Preface

THANKS ARE DUE

Great advances in modern equipment and research within the past ten years have made greenhouse gardening easier for beginner and professional alike. My own experience should prove, beyond all shadow of doubt, that anyone can quickly learn to garden well enough in a greenhouse to grow flowers and plants all year round, and have a lot of fun doing it. *The New Greenhouse Gardening for Everyone* includes the latest information on material and equipment for growing plants under glass. But no account could be up to date without help from those who continually work in the interest of better greenhouse gardening.

Special thanks go to A. W. Dimock, Kenneth Post, John Naegele, and Harold Gray of Cornell University; O. W. Davidson of Rutgers University; D. C. Kiplinger of Ohio State University; Clark Thayer of Massachusetts State College; M. Truman Fossum of the U. S. Dept. of Agriculture; Prof. Alex Laurie, of Eustis, Fla.; T. E. King and Burnham Bowden of Lord & Burnham.

Others to whom I owe a debt of gratitude for furnishing the latest data and checking portions of the manuscript are E. J. Alexander and T. H. Everett of the New York Botanical Garden; F. F. Rockwell and Montague Free of Flower Grower Magazine; Fred Lindeman of the Men's Garden Club of New York; Dr. Harold E. Anthony of the American Museum of Natural History; Helen Van Pelt Wilson, Fairfield, Conn.; E. S. Boerner of Jackson and Perkins; Rod McLellan of South San Francisco, Calif.; Yoder Bros. of Barberton, Ohio; Scott E. Haselton of the Cactus and Succulent Society of America; and my secretary, Irene Baranowski.

And still more, am I indebted to the Johns, Joes, and Jerrys, the hundreds of unsung professional gardeners, growers, and amateurs who have so kindly and freely given of their practical experience. If I am able to pass the help they gave me to others, this book will serve its purpose.

In preparing this book, Liberty Hyde Bailey's *Hortus Second* has been my guide and authority, and in some cases names of newer introductions are from the originators' lists and catalogs.

ERNEST CHABOT

Editor's Foreword

A pleasant aspect of modern gardening is the increasing opportunity to grow plants under glass. Once greenhouses were only for the wealthy; today prices have been scaled down to the man of modest means who can in this how-to-do-it era put up his own greenhouse. Frames made of aluminum make the superstructure light to handle and considerably reduce upkeep. Modern contrivances for automatic operation take into account the busy gardener's limited or intermittent hours. Heating, shading, ventilating, even watering can now go on in absentia.

With such conveniences, more and more men—and women—have turned to greenhouse gardening, as witness the tremendous popularity of Ernest Chabot's first book for the amateur. It was published in 1946 by Barrows and went through seven large printings including one revision.

By 1955, there was so much more to tell that a brand-new text was indicated, and also fresh illustration and more in color. So here is *The New Greenhouse Gardening for Everyone.* In it, the author answers all the questions greenhouse gardeners have been asking him in the last

9

nine years. He fully describes all the improvements for gardening under glass. He tells how to grow some 600 plants. He even indicates ways and means of making your hobby pay.

No one, of course, could be better informed on the subject. Ernest Chabot has long enjoyed a greenhouse of his own where he started gardening under glass with just as little knowledge as anyone with a first greenhouse. Through the years, as an executive of a large greenhouse concern, he has been in direct contact with buyers. Thus he knows their problems—and in this book he solves them. Barrows is therefore particularly gratified to be able to offer to greenhouse enthusiasts so up-to-date a book with such a simple, authentic text as *The New Greenhouse Gardening for Everyone*.

HELEN VAN PELT WILSON

Gardening Made Easy

THERE IS NO END to the possibilities for fun, flowers, and plants in a modern home greenhouse. Winter snows and cold storms may rage, but your garden under glass is oblivious to it. There are flowers for cutting, bulbs opening their blooms, pot plants crowned with buds all ready to burst into a spectacle of beauty. Your old favorites along with newly acquired treasures reach a higher degree of perfection than you ever imagined.

The best results under glass take less time and effort —much less than in outdoor gardening. Everything essential to healthy plant growth is under your control—temperature, humidity, soil moisture, light, nutrients, and ventilation. You don't have to kneel or stoop to cultivate your plants for they are grown on raised benches and shelves. All your tools and potting and storage facilities are within easy reach. Weeds, insects, burning sunshine, drying winds, and storms are no problem. Heat and ventilation are thermostatically controlled. Even watering can be semiautomatic, so you can leave your greenhouse for weeks unattended. This is gardening at its best!

Greenhouse Plants for Beginners

Like most of us starting out with a new greenhouse, you may feel a little timid when selecting plants to grow. But I assure you no superspecial knowledge or skill is needed as many beginners seem to think; at least that's the way it was with me. You soon find that beginners with bright new greenhouses, have the biggest show. Why? Because at first it's just natural to choose plants with which you are familiar—azaleas, geraniums, tulips, primroses, pansies, and simple, outdoor-garden cut flower varieties that can't be beat for abundant blooms. All are yours in gay succession—just for the growing. (See cool greenhouse plants listed in the calendar in Chapter 23.)

You'll find the good old stand-bys untempermental as to temperature changes, drafts, and intermittent sunshine, yet sure-fire for the greatest splash of color during the seasons when you want it.

"Won't they prove commonplace and stuffy?" you ask. Not unless you have a special yen for the rare and unusual. But that fascinating story follows later. The list is long, widely varied, and highlighted by new introductions and additions each year. Bench space will prove your big limitation, but here is a beginners' schedule many of my friends and I use for a gay parade of flowers throughout the year. The average dimensions of the greenhouses we have are 10 feet wide by 16 to 20 feet long.

Fall. Fill the greenhouse with chrysanthemums. Select early, mid-season, and late varieties for the boldest show well into January. So vastly different are the sizes, colors, and forms, there is no lack of variety in bloom for display or cutting.

Midwinter. You will appreciate the greenhouse more than ever during this season. Even before the chrysanthemums taper off, daffodils and early tulips are in flower. These occupy the shelves together with anemones and ranunculus. Plants of snapdragons, calendulas, fragrant stock, and perhaps sweet peas, that have been growing in pots, are put in just as soon as bench space is available.

Late Winter and Early Spring. The greenhouse fairly glows in reds, yellows, lavenders, pinks, and blues. The annuals mentioned above have come into full flower. There are more daffodils, Darwin and Parrot tulips, Wedgwood iris, hyacinths, and lilies in white and rainbow shades.

Spring and Early Summer. The bulb blooms continue right through April, but annual chrysanthemums or marguerites, and Boston yellow daisies, along with a second crop of snapdragons and calendula, provide cut flowers. Of course, you might want carnations, delphiniums or cornflowers instead.

You may also enjoy really early tomatoes along with radishes, lettuce, and other greens. In late spring, you will be starting plants for the outdoor garden. It's one of the most profitable things to do in the greenhouse. Thousands of plants can be raised in a comparatively small area at very low cost.

Summer. There is no time more ideal than summer to grow many plants under glass. Asters and carnations for example, do ever so much better in a greenhouse than outdoors. This is true of all plants vulnerable to insect attack, burning sunshine, or driving wind and rain. Melons do particularly well. Golden-fleshed fruit up to six or seven pounds is possible. Then there are many summer-flowering pot plants such as fragrant jasmines, colorful clerodendrum, and plumbago, just to mention a few. But as usual you must conserve space, for by August and September you will again be starting chrysanthemums and a host of seedlings for winter bloom.

You may think it takes a lot of time to have flowers in succession all year. Most of us do it in five or six hours a week—twenty minutes to water each morning and three or four hours to garden on week ends. With automatic watering, you would take still less time. But you must maintain a planting schedule. Varieties of plants with a short life-span that ends after flowering must be kept coming along all the time, so there will be a new crop to replace the old.

Schedule for the Busy Person

Don't think you can't enjoy a greenhouse because you don't have time. There are ever so many flowering and foliage plants that are easily grown with a little attention. Established plants of the varieties listed in the tables and calendars for moderate or warm temperatures are of this type. Some can be grown on for three or four years and more, without even needing repotting. A yearly top-dressing will do. Some of my plants don't get that, yet flower beautifully year after year with no attention other than watering, periodic fumigation, and liquid feeding. The good preparations we have today make it all so simple. Even orchids are easier to grow and take much less time than you imagine.

The Single-Plant Greenhouse

The fascinating flowers and plants you can grow are practically unlimited. The romance of the orchid, for example, is as alluring as any best-seller or mystery story. Do you know that there are over a half-million hybrids with more coming along each year? In addition to orchids, you will grow other exotics with both striking foliage and attractive blooms. Weird bulb blooms from the depths of South Africa, flowering shrubs from the jungles of South America and India—you can go on and on exploring one group after another, year in and year out, and never finish following their enchanting trail. If you have a fondness for one particular group of plants, you'll enjoy specializing.

While orchids are most popular by actual survey, African violets run a close second. There are ever so many alluring varieties. Never has any plant met with such widespread enthusiasm in so short a time. Hundreds of thousands of plants are grown each year. Three years ago, the wife of one of my friends preferred a new greenhouse to a fur coat just to grow them. Now she has 300 different kinds and has bought two fur coats by selling surplus plants!

And speaking of selling plants and flowers, there are many who supplement their annual income this way. It's a splendid idea, especially after retirement. Earnings range from $500 to $4,000 and more. (See also Chapter 22.) If you grow orchids, you will soon meet many a fan who sells his extra blooms. Others may sell house plants, husky seedlings to set out each spring, corsages, and so on.

Geraniums are also widely grown both for blooms and foliage. One of my friends has 298 different varieties. Camellias are still another possibility, and they present a magnificent sight when 150 to 200 blooms crowd a single plant. They are excellent to cut and float in bowls or to use for corsages.

There are cacti enthusiasts, too, although at first you may find it difficult to appreciate what anyone sees in them. At least that's how it was with me. Then, instead of thorny, hard-surfaced plants, I became aware of a certain kind of beauty in the symmetrical pattern and brilliant flowers of these plants that thrive on desert and plain as nothing else will.

Other plants for specialties include alpines, begonias, lilies, bromeliads, fuchsias, amaryllis, and collections of unique South African bulb plants. If you haven't a particular favorite, perhaps the thing to do is try a few of several groups until you find one. Naturally you run the chance of developing a fondness for so many plants that it would take a greenhouse a block long to house them all. But like the rest of us whose interests are equally wide, you'll continue to look for more plants to "conquer."

2

Your New Greenhouse

A GREENHOUSE IS NO LONGER a luxury which only a millionaire can afford. Anyone can have one of fine design for the cost of a good secondhand car. The latest models have wide panes of glass on a strong, slender framework to admit maximum light, and they can be adequately ventilated to provide the best conditions for any crop in any climate.

Modern materials and manufacturing methods have made it possible to produce greenhouses in a lower price range. Prefabricated models, which most home gardeners set up themselves, save a lot in construction costs. The parts go together so simply, you don't need men skilled in carpentry, masonry, painting, glazing, or steam fitting to do the work. There are no parts to cut. Everything, including the angular glass for the ends, is cut to fit into place.

Greenhouses with an all-aluminum framework, and those of California redwood with aluminum barcaps, are bright, trim-looking, and maintenance-free. Neither type ever needs a protective coat of paint, although a linseed-oil rub will bring out the color of redwood. No putty is necessary. In the best types the glass is set in rubber or plastic strips and sealed outside with aluminum barcaps. Bolts, screws, hinges, and all other fastenings are aluminum or stainless steel, not coated or electroplated. There is nothing to rust out or wear out.

Masonry work is simplified, too, through special kits. Only a few shovelfuls of cement are needed for post-hole footings and cement piers. Greenhouse sills are set on steel posts and you can apply whatever siding material you want—clapboard, waterproof plywood, smooth or corrugated asbestos-cement board, glass brick, or even plastic in the warmer southern states. Of course, footings and foundation must extend below the frostline to prevent heaving through alternate freezing and thawing. This is especially important for attached greenhouses.

If cinder block is used, apply a coat of stucco to cover up the joints. Of course with concrete block, poured concrete, or brick, steel posts are not needed. In no case should the careful treatment of greenhouse walls be neglected, for they are the one opaque part of the structure and most important to its good looks.

Ventilation

Large-sized roof ventilators in new type greenhouses are manipulated by easy-working arm-and-rod operators and jack gears. In less expensive houses, push rods are used.

Automatic roof ventilation is the greatest of modern conveniences for the home greenhouse gardener. All that is necessary is to set a thermostat, and electric-driven motors operate the sash as required. You can leave your greenhouse day after day without giving the ventilators a thought because they open automatically when it becomes too warm and close if it turns cool.

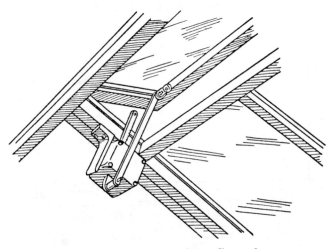

Automatic ventilation for the small greenhouse.

In small greenhouses, individual motors, as pictured, operate the apparatus, but in conventional type greenhouses with 29-inch-wide sash, a big motor-operator with a modulating thermostat is used.

Slanted, Straight-Sided, and Curved-Eave Greenhouses

There is a wide variety of standard styles and sizes in greenhouses to choose from. Dutch light models with sides slanted to the sun, and types with straight sides or graceful eaves are made in free-standing, connected, and lean-to styles.

The most popular prefabricated style greenhouse has

sides slanted to catch the direct rays of the winter sunshine. There are other advantages, too. It has height without appearing to be high, and is self-supporting without inside cross ties or columns. Heat is less expensive

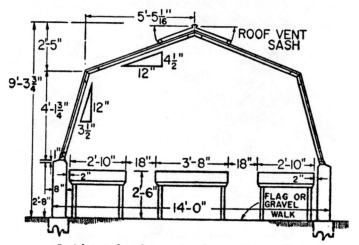

Prefabricated angle-eave greenhouse, 14 feet wide.

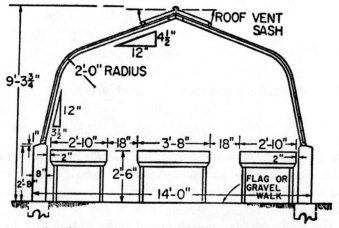

Prefabricated curved-eave greenhouse, 14 feet wide.

because there is less glass surface for the area covered, for the more glass the more heat loss. (See Chapter 3.)

Those who prefer greenhouses with straight sides point out that tall plants can be grown close to the glass, but the slight angle in the sides of modern slant-sided types leaves ample headroom for the average plant grown.

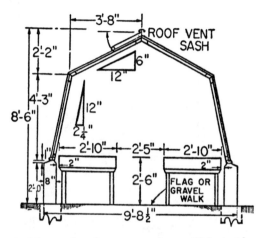

Prefabricated angle-eave greenhouse, 10 feet wide.

Curved-eave greenhouses with long sweeping, graceful lines blend well with any home or garden setting. There is a clear span of glass from the sill up—nothing to cast shade or obstruct the view.

Connected vs. Free-Standing Greenhouse

A connected or attached greenhouse often becomes the most popular room in the house. It is not only a delightful spot to grow and enjoy your favorite flowers, but a place for entertaining friends, a solarium in which to soak up health-giving sun, or a quiet hideaway for re-

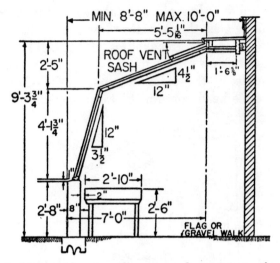

Prefabricated lean-to angle-eave greenhouse, 9 feet wide.

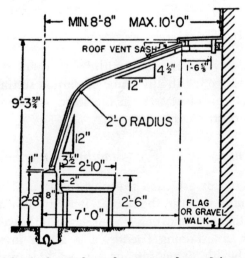

Prefabricated curved-eave lean-to greenhouse, 9 feet wide.

A lean-to greenhouse fits attractively into a setback between two wings of the house where it can be enjoyed from a number of rooms, both upstairs and down. (Lord & Burnham Photo)

(*Above*) An all-aluminum prefabricated lean-to greenhouse of the sectional type. It is extra roomy — takes two 2-foot benches. (*Below*) A light and airy lean-to greenhouse with extra-wide glass and a frame of aluminum. (Gotscho-Schleisner Photos)

(*Above*) Built with casement-sash, this lean-to greenhouse is harmonious with many styles of architecture. (*Below*) The site was excavated for this lean-to and the walls lowered so as to continue the graceful line of the roof — one of the most attractive greenhouses of this type that I have ever seen. (Lord & Burnham Photos)

(*Above*) It is easy to construct a prefabricated greenhouse. The all-aluminum sections go together like this, and are joined with stainless-steel fastenings. (*Below*) This budget-priced greenhouse is made of natural-finish California redwood. The staging lines soften the foundation attractively. (Lord & Burnham Photos)

laxation. It will be used much more than a free-standing greenhouse in the garden.

A connected greenhouse with an even span of glass on both sides has many advantages over a lean-to type. It provides better growing conditions because it extends out farther from the house and so more glass is exposed to sun. Plants are lighted more evenly from all directions and don't have to lean toward the sun. There is also more growing area for your money.

Of course, frequently because of limited space or the desire for harmony with a particular architectural style, a lean-to fits in best. Don't build a tiny one, though. It will be difficult to maintain an even temperature because there will not be enough volume of air. The temperature rises and falls with the sun and drops quickly as the sun goes down. A large opening or doorway into the house is helpful. It cuts down the wall space, which absorbs the heat of the sun, and provides an extra amount of air to act as a cushion against rapid temperature changes. At night the lean-to may be closed off from the house with a door or a screen.

Location

Place the greenhouse where it will get the most sun, especially morning light in winter when the arc of the sun is low. Plant development is strongest during early morning after the long night rest so light after 3:00 P.M. (S.T.) is not too important. With greenhouses of extra-wide panes which we have today, it makes little difference whether the ridge runs east and west, north and south, or anywhere in between. Experts once advised the best placement was on a line drawn 10 degrees N.E.

This may well be true of old-type houses with narrow glass and bulky structural members.

Connected greenhouses are best located on the south or southeast side of a building. A west or even a north exposure may be satisfactory for growing orchids, African violets, foliage plants, and other tropicals that want diffused light.

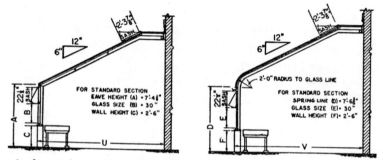

Angle-eave lean-to greenhouse.   *Curved-eave lean-to greenhouse.*

Conventional Lean-to Greenhouses. Dimensions given in figures are fixed. Those lettered are variable to suit conditions at the site. Widths are usually one half of a standard greenhouse but may be increased by widening the flat deck to suit requirements.

Sometimes windows and doors create a problem in connecting a greenhouse to a building. This may usually be overcome by increasing the wall height so the openings come inside the greenhouse, or by excavating to lower the greenhouse floor so the roof comes below the windows.

The greenhouse should be placed out of the range of falling branches, ice, and snow. Where necessary, a single snow guard can be placed on the house roof above a connected greenhouse. This is merely a pipe which runs along the eave of the building. Screens of galvanized wire-cloth are sometimes a necessary protection over part of the glass.

Size and Proportions

Choosing a greenhouse that is too small is a very common error. On paper, and even when first completed,

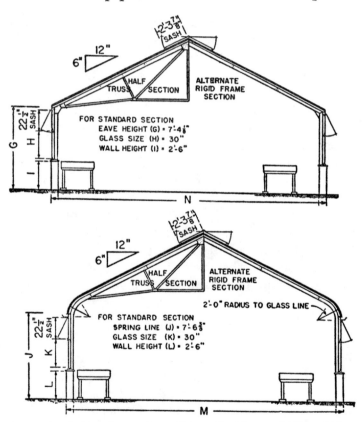

Conventional Greenhouse Construction, Straight- and Curved-Eave Types, with complete steel frame. Standard widths are 18 feet; 21 feet, 6 inches; and 25 feet. Lengths are in bays of 8 feet, 7¾ inches. Other dimensions given in letters are variable to suit conditions at the site.

the greenhouse may appear large, and you wonder how you are ever going to fill it; but no matter how large it is, this always takes care of itself. You fill the benches, load the shelves, hang plants from the roof, put them in the walks and still need more space. Then you ask yourself, "Why didn't I build it large enough?"

Prefabricated types can be extended quite easily. The addition of an extra compartment, heated to a different temperature, makes it possible to grow a wider variety of plants.

The greenhouse should not be too large for you to take care of, unless you intend to have help. One 10 or 15 feet wide by 20 feet long can easily be handled during a few hours a week, especially if it is equipped for automatic ventilation.

It is economical to build a greenhouse in good proportions. A structure 8 by 8 feet with two benches costs more per square foot than one 14 feet wide by 18 feet long with three benches. There is good reason for this. The glass ends, sides, ventilating sash and operators are the most expensive parts of the greenhouse, yet do not cover any space. The size of the greenhouse can be increased without materially affecting the cost of these items.

Conventional Greenhouse Construction

You can still put up a greenhouse the old custom-built way with individual parts such as glazing bars, posts, sills, purlins, eave plates and ridge. Manufacturers offer such materials "framed" or cut to fit, but even the best require skill in carpentry and glazing to erect. There is much squaring and leveling to do. Every part must be set to exact measurement with bars perfectly parallel and at right angles to the ridge, eave, and sills. Otherwise, glass which has square corners will not fit the openings and each light may have to be cut separately.

Putty glazing is also a problem to the layman. The glass is set or bedded in putty—not surface puttied as with windows. Surface putty would soon dry up and wash away and, unless protected with aluminum barcaps, the putty seam must be sealed with paint every three or four years. Manufacturers' catalogs show how to do this.

Secondhand or homemade greenhouse materials are seldom satisfactory. By the time you have sawed out rotted wood, scraped away old paint, putty, nails, chipped glass, and rust, you'll wish you had bought new material. Homemade materials usually rot out or are unsatisfactory because they are not enduring and not functionally right.

California redwood is excellent structural material for a greenhouse, if the wood is carefully selected and nails, bolts, screws, and other fastenings are of hot galvanized or stainless steel, or aluminum. An acid in the wood soon causes plated and coated fastenings and adjacent wood to disintegrate.

The clear heartwood of swamp-grown cypress is excellent, too, but expensive and scarce. Upland cypress and kinds containing sapwood rot within five years and are not satisfactory. In the end, as with everything else, you get just what you pay for. The cost of masonry, glass, benches, and heating are the same for all greenhouses so the difference in price between a good prefabricated greenhouse and a homemade job is very little.

Whenever you can, choose a greenhouse of standard size. Prices for special dimensions and custom designs are more than triple the cost of standard models. It is best to use your own ingenuity in fitting a construction of standard size to suit the site. Unless the design is extremely involved, it can often be built with simple homemade filler-pieces or glass panels.

Plastic vs. Glass

You may wonder why plastics aren't used in place of glass. The big reason is plastics cost five times more than glass and the products available today are not altogether suitable. Fiberglas polyesters are translucent and admit only 82 per cent of available light when new. This is satisfactory for certain crops such as orchids, African violets, and similar tropicals, but other flowering plants want full sunlight. Since the plastic is corrugated to give it necessary strength, there is certain to be some condensation drip. The material is opaque or translucent so impossible to see through.

Acrylic plastics have a bright surface and, when new, their light transmission may be approximately the same as glass. The sheets will continue to transmit light for four or five years before repolishing is needed. Watch for progress, however. Eventually, we may have a suitable glass substitute.

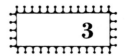

3

Greenhouse Heating

In selecting the best type of heat for your green-house, consider its size, your particular location, and the fuel service available. Fortunately, modern equipment simplifies heating, especially with the tightly sealed bar-capped greenhouses of today.

It must be remembered that a greenhouse is not a "hot house." Many of the finest flowers, as well as a number of vegetables, do not want a night temperature higher than 40 to 50°. Blooms are of better quality, insects are less bothersome, and fuel bills are much lower, when you grow plants "cool." Even warm-temperature plants such as orchids, African violets and other tropicals want night temperatures of only 70 to 75°. (See recommended temperatures for individual plants listed in Chapters 7 to 14, and 23.)

If you have a small lean-to or a greenhouse connected to the house, the heat that passes through a large door or window may be adequate. Sometimes an opening or flue from the ceiling of a warm cellar can be used with a thermostatically controlled electric fan in the green-house to circulate the warm air. Adequate heat at even temperatures is essential to success, and a larger green-house, even if connected to the house, requires a separate heater or system.

If possible, install thermostatically controlled heat and ventilation. Plant quality will be higher with much less care, and fuel costs will be lower.

Ordinary house-heating thermostats should not be used in the greenhouse for moisture will corrode the contacts. Use the mercury-tube type with contacts en-closed in a glass tube—they are moisture-proof.

The amount of radiation needed for a greenhouse is also different from that for house heating. The large glass surface makes a rapid pick-up necessary to com-pensate for the sudden drop in temperature when the sun goes down at night and artificial heat takes over. There must also be adequate capacity for the coldest of windy nights, even though they may be few and far between. Your greenhouse builder is experienced in these matters so it is wise to consult him.

The electric, oil, or natural gas space heaters used should be the type with a built-in fan that uses little current. Heat is wanted down near the floor. Otherwise, you may have a greenhouse with a "hot head" and "warm feet." Oil and natural gas fired boilers or heaters can be placed right in the greenhouse. Boilers and fur-naces burning artificial gas or coal *must* be located in a separate building—the fumes are death to plant life.

Electric Heating Units

It is most convenient and practical to heat a greenhouse with electricity using 2 or 4 kilowatt unit heaters. Heat is clean, one hundred per cent efficient, and completely automatic. Current comes on at the precise instant the thermostat calls for heat and shuts off when the desired temperature is reached.

Electric heat is also excellent to supplement another type heater that furnishes most of the warmth. If for example, the oil or gas heater used is not adequate for cold nights, the electric unit can be set to turn on when needed.

Temperature control will be even and automatic when warm air is circulated by a small built-in electric fan. The heater is usually set under a bench or at the end of a walk, but when more than one is needed, they should be placed in opposite corners of the greenhouse.

Wiring should always be done by an electrician. It should extend in a separate circuit to the meter and must be large enough to carry the load.

Costwise, electric heat is practical for the cool greenhouse (45 to 50°), especially when rates drop as low as 2 to 2½ cents per kilowatt. The cost of heating my 13- by 18-foot greenhouse to 50° at night ran $150 a season. This is at 2 cents per kilowatt, the rate after the usual $8.00 is used for light, refrigeration, and other appliances. Naturally, most of the cost is during January and February when 50 to 60 per cent of the current for the entire heating season is used.

Natural or Bottled Gas Heat

If natural gas is available, heating is economical. Be sure the utility company never mixes in artificial gas. Even with a closed-flame heater, the fumes are sure death to plant life. Most gas companies know this and will never run artificial gas lines anywhere near a greenhouse.

Bottled gas (liquid petroleum, propane, or butane gas) is also suitable and economical in most localities. The suppliers now set up permanent tanks and will connect your heater for a nominal fee. Gas is metered as used, and delivered periodically just as with oil. The unsightly tanks can be camouflaged with paint and concealed in shrubbery.

The gas is burned in an ordinary space heater, but must be vented. The vent cannot be run through the roof of the greenhouse for either excessive or inadequate draft will snuff out the flame. Such heaters work only when installed with a tall brick chimney as in a house.

One type of gas heater, known as the Safe-Aire has proven satisfactory in greenhouse heating throughout the country. It is installed in an aluminum panel substituted for a light of glass at the greenhouse end. No chimney is needed because the gas is burned in a sealed chamber with all products of combustion separated from the greenhouse air. This is a safeguard against plant damage by fumes so frequent when unvented heaters are used.

Oil Heaters

Suitable oil heaters that burn distillate kerosene or No. 2 fuel oil are available through mail order catalogs and from local appliance dealers. Control can be thermostatic or by hand. Some trade names are Coleman, Florence, Mayflower, Perfex and Duo-Therm. Greenhouse manufacturers will recommend the size heater needed.

Distillate oil is available in most rural areas, but it is wise to check first with fuel suppliers. Oil manufactured by the catalytic-cracking process smokes so much that it clogs pilot light and flues in the heater.

Hot Water Heat

A hot water heating system with oil burner, natural gas, or stoker is the most dependable for the home greenhouse. Heat is steady and not subject to sudden fluctuations. Black steel pipe along the walls is often used for radiation but fin tubing is better, for it is more convenient to install and takes less room. One line is equivalent to three to five of pipe. Such a system can be connected to the house heating boiler, whether it is hot water or steam, or to a separate boiler as described later.

Extending a House-Heating Steam System. Most house boilers usually have sufficient surplus to take care of the greenhouse, especially since the house doesn't need heat at night when the greenhouse does. *A* and *C* are draw-off cocks for draining the system. *B* and *D* are check valves which are not needed if the boiler is on the greenhouse floor level. *E* is an air vent to release air when filling the system, or to vent any air pockets that may form.

Gate valves are at *F* for closing off the greenhouse system. Flow-and-return mains run from the boiler to the greenhouse radiation. The flow line is connected to a tap below the water line in the boiler. If the boiler is

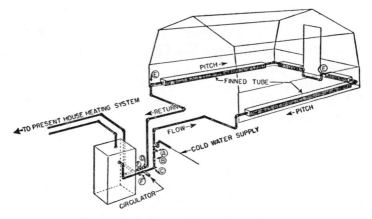

Extension of a House-Heating Steam System.

the type with dry nipples, that is, with the water line below the nipples, a header tapped into each section is needed. An electric circulator in the flow main pumps hot water to the radiation. A thermostat in the greenhouse starts the pump the instant heat is needed and turns it off when the desired temperature has been reached. An aquastat regulates the water temperature when the house is not using heat.

For economy in running and insulating the mains, the greenhouse should be located within 100 feet of the boiler. If mains are run underground, place them below frost and insulate them well. A good tunnel can be made of 8-inch soil pipe. Joints should be sealed with cement to keep out water.

Extending a House-Heating Hot Water System. With a modern forced hot water heating system, the installation of mains and greenhouse radiation is similar to the extension of the steam system, but the flow main is from the top of the boiler and the return to the bottom, with the circulator in the return main. The greenhouse system is zoned separately from the house with its own greenhouse thermostat and circulator.

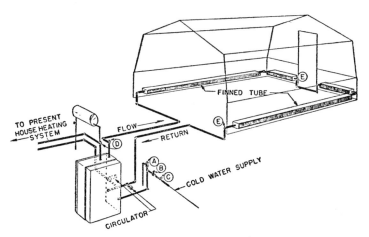

Extension of a House-Heating Hot Water System.

The boiler could either be on a grade, as shown, or in a cellar. *A* is a pressure relief valve; *B* is a pressure reducing valve; *C* is a globe valve; *D* is a flow control valve; *E* indicates air vents. Old type hot water systems with water temperatures lower than 180° can be adapted, too, but require more radiation in the greenhouse.

Extending a Hot Air System. If your house is heated by hot air, two ducts may be extended into the connected greenhouse to furnish heat, as illustrated. Both ducts are installed close to the floor and operation is independent of the house heat. An electric fan or blower is installed in one duct in connection with a thermostat in the green-

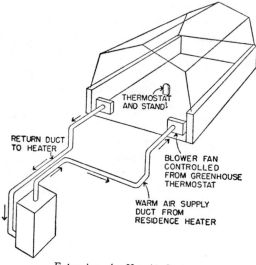

THERMOSTAT
AND STAND

RETURN DUCT
TO HEATER

BLOWER FAN
CONTROLLED
FROM GREENHOUSE
THERMOSTAT

WARM AIR SUPPLY
DUCT FROM
RESIDENCE HEATER

Extension of a Hot Air System.

house which actuates the blower and burner control in the heater. Cool air is returned by the other duct.

Heat from a Separate Boiler

The initial cost of a boiler, complete with an oil or natural gas burner and a hot water heating system, is more expensive. The cost may run as high as the greenhouse itself, but is worth it when you plan to grow valuable plants or intend to sell the surplus.

Such systems are sold in complete units so anyone with a yen to do-it-himself can install them. The systems are equipped with a circulator so the boiler can be set in a corner of the greenhouse or in a nearby workroom or garage. Temperature control is most accurate because the water in the boiler is always very hot—200 to 210°.

There is a smaller volume of water to circulate, especially with fin radiation. The system heats fast in the evening when the outside temperature takes its sudden drop. It cools faster when the sun comes up in the morning too, for the thermostat stops the circulator.

Another great advantage is that a cast iron steam boiler is used and steam can be valved from it whenever wanted for sterilization of soil. Tempered water for watering and hot water for washing pots is also available.

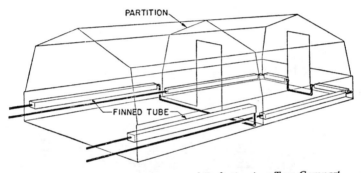

Arrangement of Pipe Connections and Radiation in a Two-Compartment Greenhouse.

Two-Compartment Greenhouse. In a two-compartment greenhouse, you can grow a much wider variety of plants. The diagram shows the proper arrangement of pipe connections and radiation. The cool compartment is usually 50° and farthest from the boiler; the warmer compartment is usually 55 to 60°, or 65 to 75°, depending upon the plants grown.

Gravity Hot Water System. An inexpensive type of gravity hot water system is installed with the boiler in a cellar or pit. Frequently, a domestic hot water heater, laundry stove, or similar small boiler is used. The lowest point of the coils in the greenhouse must be higher than the water line in the boiler to insure circulation, and the deeper the boiler cellar, the faster the circulation. An expansion tank located at the highest point of the system is needed.

The pipe coils are made up of 1½- or 2-inch black steel pipe located near the floor of the greenhouse. Pipes are spaced apart to insure free circulation of air around them. The sketch shows the proper relation of boiler, coils, connections, and expansion tank.

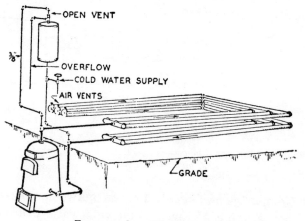

Economical small house system.

(Left) A convenient greenhouse workroom with built-in sink, potting bench, soil bin.

(Center) A workroom of simple frame construction, unfinished stained walls.

This workroom has a more elaborate novelty ceiling finish, large potting bench, pot racks, soil bins. (Lord & Burnham Photos)

(Left) A shelf makes a handy arrangement for tools in a small greenhouse. They are held in place with steel clips. *(Below)* A portable potting tray is convenient to use indoors or out.

(Below) The greenhouse fumigator is lit with a sparkler. Fumigation is an excellent means of keeping the greenhouse free of insects. (Author Photos)

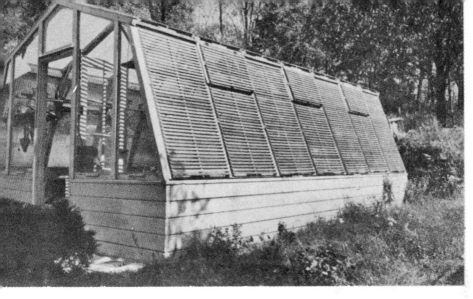

(*Above*) Slat shades are made in panels so they can be easily slipped on and off the greenhouse. (Lord & Burnham Photo) (*Below*) Vinyl plastic provides an easy and inexpensive way to waterproof a wood bench. (Author Photo)

This pit house with glass sides provides better growing conditions than one with solid sides. Roof is of hot-bed sash. Interior view is shown at left. Roof is supported with pipe columns and purlins. Side sash can be opened for ventilation. (See Chapter 21)

(Below) An excellent greenhouse for storing valuable shrubs and perennials throughout the winter. Note vent sash in walls. (Eric Baker Photos)

Greenhouse Equipment

Good working facilities contribute immeasurably to the success and enjoyment of a greenhouse. You need a place to pot plants, sow seeds, prepare soil, and do the many interesting things connected with year-round gardening.

It's grand to have a separate garden house or workroom, as described later. If like most of us, you have a single-compartment free-standing greenhouse, you will arrange to do your work in the northwest corner. In this spot, any cabinets or racks you may set up will not cast shade or encroach materially on valuable growing space. Your soil and pots can be stored underneath the plant benches. Waterproof this section of bench with a sheet of vinyl plastic, waterproof plywood or similar material, so water will not drip below.

Make a soil bin by nailing 1-inch boards across pairs of bench legs to form a back and two sides. Place the boards for the front between cleats so they can be removed individually as the soil pile goes down. Make a pot rack

41

with slats nailed horizontally across two pairs of bench legs. Stack pots of the same size together.

A cabinet or small closet with shelves or hinged doors is easily made for seed, fertilizers, and small tools. The doors can be of plywood, masonite, or similar material. The doors of the cabinet itself, or a piece of plywood

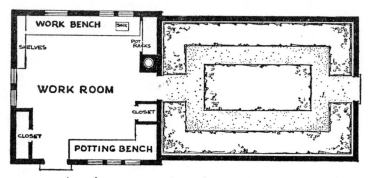

A good arrangement of greenhouse with workroom.

nailed to the edge of a plant shelf, make a good tool rack. Use spring steel clips and hooks to hang the tools so they can be picked out and replaced quickly.

The Potting Bench

Make the potting bench of heavy lumber tightly fitted together. It must be able to take plenty of pounding and there can be no cracks for soil to seep through. A good size would be the width of the plant bench, usually 2 feet 10 inches by 3 to 4 feet long. Make the bottom of ½- to ⅝-inch waterproof plywood or tongue-and-groove flooring. Brace this underneath with two-by-threes. The boards for the sides and back should be 6 inches high to let you pile up soil without its sliding off.

The Potting Tray

Where space is at a premium, a potting tray can replace the bench. The tray is built like the potting bench described above but has no legs. When needed, it is set temporarily on a plant bench or over the walk between two plant benches. At other times, it is stored under a bench.

Tools

In selecting tools, the moist air in the greenhouse must be considered. Choose stainless steel or galvanized steel and possibly copper. Electro and cadmium plating on tools is useless in resisting rust. Aluminum isn't good either because it disintegrates in contact with soil—especially soil that has been limed.

A good sharp stainless-steel knife is a useful tool in the greenhouse. It is needed for taking cuttings, pruning, and many other jobs. You will also need a good pair of shears. Those resembling small tin snips are best. They are sturdier and better suited than scissors.

For watering and syringing, you will want a bulb, watering can, and hose. A long-spouted watering can is handy in a small greenhouse for watering plants under benches. Fine and coarse roses are needed.

A hose of light plastic is now available and is excellent for greenhouse use because it is so easy to move about. A hose nozzle is not generally used in greenhouses, but I like one type which has a lever hand-control for turning water on and off instantly, and a long spout of small diameter which makes it easy to avoid wetting the foliage of soft plants. For syringing and watering seed flats, this nozzle can be replaced with one that produces a fine mist.

It's hard to find a good sprayer. I use one of the bucket type that works rather well. Some of my friends have foreign-made hand sprayers but they have only a one-quart capacity. Of course, a motor-driven power operator that gets up to 150 pounds pressure would be ideal but rather expensive.

Dibble and potting sticks are best made of hardwood such as ash or oak; soil does not stick so readily to their dense grained surfaces. An excellent small plastic dibble is now available. A flat three-cornered mason's trowel is useful for scraping, tamping, leveling, and marking off soil.

Shop tools such as screw drivers, pliers and a hammer come in for almost daily use. A small can of light oil is a must for lubricating motors and ventilating equipment, as well as for oiling tools.

The best cultivator is one you can make yourself. It is merely a sharp-pointed single hook fitted into a file handle. Stiff wire bent into two prongs make light cultivators which are perfect for cultivating seedlings in flats or loosening soil of potted plants.

Other small items you will want to have handy include a stiff brush for cleaning up the potting bench, spoons for measuring, sieves of $\frac{1}{16}$-, $\frac{1}{8}$- and $\frac{1}{4}$-inch mesh, a hardwood tamping block, a wooden slat sharpened along one edge for leveling and marking, and possibly a spotting board for marking off seedlings. A good one can be made with the prongs of a discarded wooden rake. A large wooden scoop is handy for moving soil from bin to work bench. A 6-inch strainer with handle, like the one used in the kitchen, is handy for many things.

Rubber gloves might be wanted when handling poisonous insecticides or washing pots. You will also need pots

Tools and Supplies. They are simple and make your gardening easy.

in a series of sizes from 2½ to 8 inches. Larger-size pots are rather difficult to find. Most of us now use wooden tubs when anything larger than 10 inches is needed.

Seed flats are so expensive now that many stores do not carry them. You can make good ones in sizes to suit your own needs from old berry boxes or crates. Put them together with galvanized nails. The black nails soon rust out.

Plant Benches and Shelves

Never set up small flimsy benches or tables. Buy the practical-size prefabricated type from a greenhouse manufacturer or make your own. California redwood or a good grade of cypress are the only suitable woods to use. They are durable under conditions of moisture and should last for ten or fifteen years. Only an occasional bottom board will need to be replaced. A coat of copper-naphthenate wood preserver adds years to the life of a bench.

The sketch shows a time-tested bench design. For the

Plant bench.

sides and ends, 1- by 6-inch dressed lumber is used. The bottoms are of rough 1-inch boards with ½- by 6-inch spaces every 4 feet to allow drainage. Legs are 2 by 4 inches, notched on top to take 1- by 6-inch cross braces. Side benches are usually about 3 feet wide; center benches are 3 to 6 feet wide. Benches wider than 6 feet cannot be conveniently worked even from each side.

Asbestos cement board will last indefinitely but it is expensive, especially if you have to pay shipping costs for any distance on the heavy materials. Concrete benches poured in place, as used commercially, are impractical in the home greenhouse because the cost of building and setting up the forms for so small an area runs high.

Shelves under the eaves provide valuable extra growing space. Shelf hangers and shelving can be purchased knocked-down for most standard greenhouses. The shelves can be in double or single tiers, depending upon the height of the plants to be grown.

Brackets can also be attached to the gable ends of the greenhouse. An additional line of shelving can be hung from the ridge. Remember the more shelves there are, the more shade there will be. This is not important in spring and summer, or when crops like orchids and African violets are grown, but shade slows up growth and flowering of other plants in fall and winter.

Shading

Most plants need protection from burning sunshine. Some such as orchids, African violets, gardenias, camellias, and tropical foliage plants, need shade most of the year. Others, such as roses, asters, chrysanthemums, and tomatoes, need only a little shade at the hottest time of the year. The majority of plants want shade from early spring to fall.

Slat shades like those supplied in prefabricated kits are most practicable. They are usually of California redwood or aluminum with slats spaced ⅜ inch apart to admit filtered light. On standard home greenhouses, slat shades are made in panels the same size as the glass. Patented fasteners make them easy to set up or take down.

Similar roller-type shades with bronze couplers and fastenings are made of California redwood. These are expensive but excellent because they can be regulated quickly according to the weather. On houses for orchids and other tropical plants, shades are often set up on runners 4 to 8 inches above the roof so a cooling circulation of air can pass over the glass.

For an inexpensive roller shade, you can't beat the Japanese bamboo type from a furniture store. They won't last too long, for the string that binds the bamboo slats together rots out. Even though you have to replace them every three or four years, however, the cost is not excessive.

When additional shade is needed, one to three layers of cheesecloth can be hung inside the glass. If certain plants need more shade than others, hang the cheesecloth over that section of bench.

Whitewash makes a practical, inexpensive shade, but it is so unsightly I hope no one will use it. It usually is brushed or sprayed on the glass in spring and replaced periodically after rains wash it thin. In mid-September, it is scrubbed off. Shading compounds made of whiting in paste or powder form are available in green or white from many sources. Mix them with gasoline for a temporary shade and with linseed oil for permanence.

Where valuable plants are housed, a water curtain is frequently used to cool the glass. The water is distributed with fine nozzles at the ridge and recirculated from a reservoir or tank with a small pump.

Water and Electricity

Run the water line to the greenhouse through ½- or ⅝-inch copper tubing buried below frost. A tap on a standard pipe about 2½ feet high is handy.

You will also want a large tub or pail for washing pots and tools. A sink is a great convenience, if you have space. Select a rugged one of slate, cast iron, heavy metal or porcelain, that will withstand banging and scratching. Tepid water, which is beneficial to many plants, can be run into the greenhouse at the same time. Many of us who do not have warm water, keep a pail or tub of water in the greenhouse so it reaches the same temperature before it is used.

Electric wiring can be run in the same underground trench as the water line.

Workrooms

When the greenhouse is connected to your house, try to arrange for working space in an adjoining room. Growing space under glass soon becomes scarce so reserve as much as possible for plants. A separate garden house or workroom building can be arranged with less difficulty. Some suggestions are shown in the various illustrations. Such a building can serve several purposes. It may be a tool house, workshop, and combination garage as well. Architecturally, the building can be styled to lend character to the greenhouse and blend attractively with your house, garden, and other buildings. Leading greenhouse manufacturers are always glad to suggest designs.

Less expensive is a self-contained workroom compartment of the same construction as the greenhouse, separated from the growing compartment by a glass partition and door. A space 8 or 10 feet long and equal to the width of the greenhouse is usually large enough. It should be provided with hinged ventilation as in the greenhouse, and a solid roof of asbestos cement board, composition shingles, or other suitable material for protection from the sun.

5

How to Grow Quality Plants

THE BEGINNER with good supplies and equipment
has no trouble raising blooms that approach professional
quality. A healthful atmosphere is the big thing. Ample
light, high humidity, steady temperatures, and air that
is fresh and alive are all important. Such conditions are
easily maintained, especially with thermostatically controlled heat and ventilation. It is just a case of making
adjustments according to the weather.

Watering

Most of the bugaboos about greenhouse watering stem
from books written in England for prevailing conditions
of cloudy weather. Watering is not so much of a problem
in greenhouses here, except during our periods of similar
weather, when overwatering is harmful. Soil texture influences both the amount of water needed and the fre-
quency of application. More water is required for soils
made up of coarse, loose particles; less for soils containing

large amounts of manure or other humus. Such fertile soil holds moisture and if kept soaking wet, causes soft, lush growth. Too much water drives air out of the soil so that hair roots cannot take in enough moisture to make up for the amount transpired through the leaves. Without a change of air in the soil, oxygen is exhausted and a toxic condition follows, causing root decay. Once this starts, plants rarely can be saved, even when shifted to new soil.

Gardeners who want to be on the safe side, overcome this danger by making sure soil is well drained. Large quantities of coarse sand, or even fine gravel, are added to the soil. A good soil conditioner such as Krilium, mixed one level tablespoon to an eight-quart pail of soil has the same effect. A more frequent and heavier feeding will be required by plants when a soil conditioner is used since nutrients are leached out with water.

Water your plants on bright days whenever possible. Growth is most vigorous in sunny weather when plants can take up plenty of water. Always water in the morning when temperature is rising and when the long period begins during which evaporation occurs. Condensation or water on the foliage at night is sure to cause trouble.

Be gentle with the hose or watering can. Heavy watering tends to compress the soil and drive out air. Uniform moisture throughout the root ball is the ideal condition.

Examine the soil periodically to see if moisture is needed. This is especially important in summer when gardeners have a tendency to underwater. See how much is needed by digging right down to the bottom of the bench soil with your fingers. Evaporation takes place from below as well as above. Now and then gently knock a plant out of its pot to observe drainage and condition of the soil. Pot plants frequently need more water than bench crops. Plants in small 1½- and 2-inch pots often require two or three waterings a day. Never apply water when the soil is well moistened and do not permit plants that are already wet to stand in water.

Year-round Schedule

In Fall. *Start heating system; ventilate night and day; remove shades; keep soil on dry side.* A new garden season starts during the cold, brisk days of autumn, but light is at a premium then for there are many cloudy days and the arc of the sun is very low. At this time, plants tend to make soft growth that is susceptible to mildew. Good air circulation is necessary to keep them hale and hearty.

Turn the heat on just as soon as nights become cool, and for short periods when days are damp. Keep roof ventilators open throughout the day and an inch or two at night, even though it might seem a waste of fuel. In some areas like those along our western coast, where damp weather prevails, electric fans are often used in addition to ventilators. Discontinue hosing-down walks except when the soil and air are dried out during warm bright days or by the blast of a hard-working heating system.

Furnish clean pots, seed flats, and fresh soil for the greenhouse. Winter gardening is much more pleasant and productive when supplies are ready for use. If it is necessary to wash pots and to dig up frozen clumps of soil outdoors whenever you want to sow seeds, transplant, or repot, you just won't garden when you should.

Start a new compost heap of soil, or sod and manure, for spring planting. (See Chapter 6.) The warm fall rains provide the moisture needed, and freezing and thawing throughout the winter do wonders for soil structure.

In Winter. *Avoid drafts, sudden changes in temperature, or dry, burned-out air.* Plants, like people, can't thrive in poor atmospheric conditions. In bright cold weather, it is easy to keep air fresh. Then the greenhouse traps more than enough heat from the sun, even though it may be freezing outside. Roof ventilators should be opened wide, except during very windy weather, when ventilators to windward are closed most of the way. Automatic ventilators have a half-opening stop just for this purpose. Cold down-drafts can be avoided by opening the sash halfway and tacking a layer or two of cheesecloth over the sash opening.

On cold nights, artificial heat keeps air in motion. Special adjustment is needed during long spells of cloudy weather. Drop the temperature 3 to 5° below that recommended for the crop grown, and ventilate to keep air in circulation. Leave at least a crack opening at night.

In Spring. *Increase temperature; start feeding schedule; maintain high humidity.* As days become longer and sunlight gets more intense, growth will be noticeably faster and flowering more profuse. Water daily, as required, and maintain a regular schedule of feeding. Hose-down walks and floor every morning to make up for evaporation, and to increase humidity. Night temperature may be increased as much as 5° to speed growth, especially for young seedling plants. The ideal day temperature is 10° higher, but this is impossible to maintain on hot, late spring days. Daytime temperatures may run up to 80° or more by the sun's heat although all vents and doors are open. This will not have a harmful effect. Lift or turn plants periodically to break off roots which reach through drainage holes of pots, or through the bottoms of flats. Plants will wilt and are set back materially when such roots are broken off after they have become too long.

Toward April or May shade is needed for most plants. This should be given just as soon as foliage starts to turn light green and shows signs of wilting under midday sun.

In Summer. *Increase shade; never let plants want for water; clean up, and paint.* It pays to keep the greenhouse going all summer. Plants set under shade trees in the customary way are far too likely to be neglected and suffer from dirt, drenching of summer storms, insect infestation and periods of drought. A lath house is an excellent summer shelter, but most plants can be left in the greenhouse for they are unaffected by high temperatures if sufficient moisture, shade, and humidity are maintained.

Roof ventilators should be wide open, except during storms when the half-open position is needed. Automatic roof ventilators may be disconnected and sash propped open with a block. Side ventilation is desirable for comfort while gardening, but may expel much needed humidity.

A good annual clean-up, while it is warm enough to set plants outside temporarily, pays off in quality of bloom. Remove all rubbish, dirty pots, and seed flats. Dig out weeds from under benches, scrub up benches and woodwork. Paint inside and out every third year, if necessary, using special greenhouse paint and a rust inhibitor on steel fittings. When you don't paint, fumigate while the house is empty, tripling the usual concentration.

The heating system should be cleaned at the end of the

firing season. Remove or plug up flues and chimneys—birds and squirrels find them good for nesting. Inspect and oil motors so they will be ready for use when needed.

How to Make Selections

The planting suggestions that follow and the Calendar near the end of this book give a cross-section of the groups of plants and flowers most generally grown in small- to moderate-sized greenhouses. In making selections, do not attempt to grow too many different varieties in the same greenhouse. Choose those best suited to your particular size and type of house.

Full consideration should also be given to the amount of time you will be able to devote to your plants, for gardening in the greenhouse should always be fun and never so complex as to become a burden.

The large greenhouse having several compartments heated to different temperatures, with the gardener in constant attendance, is quite another matter, but in small houses, the largest quantity and highest quality are most easily attained by selecting plants that do well under a similar system of handling.

This does not mean that you are limited entirely to plant groups requiring identical conditions of light, temperature and humidity. There can be considerable leeway within a single small greenhouse. Temperatures may vary about 5 to 10° from floor to eave, and from one end of the house to the other. A number of thermometers set in various places will quickly show the best spots for different kinds of plants.

Light intensity and humidity also may differ throughout the greenhouse and can be varied by placing select

Plants growing in pockets and crevices of a rock wall create a beautiful effect in this lean-to greenhouse built against the house. (Lord & Burnham Photo)

An attached greenhouse is more practical than a lean-to. It is easier to build, admits light from both sides and gives better control of heat and ventilation. This one is 10 by 17 feet. (Author Photo)

This curved-eave attached greenhouse blends pleasingly with most types of architecture. This one is 18 by 25 feet. Note the coldframes conveniently located against cellar windows. (Eric Baker Photo)

The attractive workroom of this 14-by-17-foot greenhouse formerly served as a garden house.

A pleasing arrangement of curved-eave greenhouse and workroom 18 by 26 feet. (Eric Baker Photos)

(Below) A handsome greenhouse with straight eaves connected to the house. It is 18 by 25 feet. (Lord & Burnham Photo)

(Above) A mixed-crop greenhouse in the springtime with tulips, cinerarias, lilies, begonias, primroses, and geraniums in full and fragrant flower. (Gottscho-Schleisner Photo) (Below) The greenhouse in blossom is a charming sight to be enjoyed a few steps down from the dining room. (Lord & Burnham Photo)

plants in a closed glass case with supplemental heat and shading. You will find some home greenhouses filled with many plants of different cultural habits doing very well together. I have seen orchids requiring a temperature of 72° growing with primroses and cyclamen that need 45 to 50°, all thriving in a small house with the thermostat set at 55°. But this does take skill and experience beyond that of the average beginner. At the start, it is best to grow plants of somewhat similar cultural needs or to build a greenhouse with two or more compartments heated to different temperatures suited to plants of diverse requirements.

In the very small greenhouse, plants such as flowering bulbs, begonias, African violets, orchids, tropical shrubs, vines, and foliage plants, growing in pots, flats, boxes, or other containers, give more fun with much less effort, than stock, snapdragons, carnations, and other cut-flower crops in benches. They are more easily shifted about, discarded, and re-grouped or replaced when they finish flowering or become dormant.

In the two- or three-bench house fifteen or more feet long, it is practical to grow flowers for cutting in benches, and have plants in pots and flats on shelves. Of course, in the small greenhouse there may not be an overabundant of blooms to cut at all times, but it is easily possible to rotate crops so there will always be something in flower. By keeping a supply of new material coming along all the time in part of the house and in garden frames, the greenhouse can be kept attractive, and you can have flowers in bloom continuously.

Much is to be gained by visits to flower shows, botanical gardens, agricultural experiment stations, florists, and greenhouses of others who garden for fun under glass.

Seeing what others are doing is a good way, also, to keep up-to-date on the finest varieties to grow.

Many of the old stand-bys suggested on the pages that follow may continue as popular greenhouse plants for years to come; others will be superseded by new varieties with something better to recommend them in one way or another. Discoveries in plant breeding, always in the making, and the continuous search in far corners of the world for suitable new varieties, keep our interest alive— an interest that makes the greenhouse a fountain of youth for all of us who love to garden under glass.

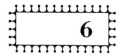

6

Soils and Fertilizers

E xperience soon teaches the greenhouse gardener how to build the best of soils. It is wonderful to have on hand all year an ample supply of a loose fibrous mixture in which roots can easily stretch out for nutrients and so produce fine plants and flowers. If you do not have time to mix soil for your first greenhouse season, garden loam can be prepared easily and will serve well. Choose a quantity of good top soil and mix in one-third as much thoroughly decomposed manure. If you cannot get cow or horse manure, the dehydrated kind will do, but use only half as much of this. Turn the mixture several times and, to avoid burning, let it stand two or three weeks before you use it.

If your soil is heavy clay, it can be loosened by adding up to 25 per cent each of peat moss or sifted leaf mold, and clean coarse sand, this in addition to the manure. If, on the other hand, your soil is very light, sandy, and porous, add the manure and some clay soil to give it body.

Superphosphate is beneficial and may be added at the

59

rate of a 3-inch potful per bushel of soil. If you do not have superphosphate on hand, add a complete 5-10-5 or 4-12-4 fertilizer at the same rate.

In no case use soil as it comes from your garden, unless it is from a special spot into which a good quantity of manure has been worked. Ordinary soil may look all right, but after a time particles break down and become compressed so they are as hard as concrete. This may occur with either heavy clay or fine sandy soil. Clay soil becomes mucky and sticky when wet; fine sandy soil becomes solidly packed. Coarse, sandy soil is not satisfactory for growing plants because it has no capacity for moisture retention. Its particles are so loose that water runs right through them.

Good soil contains a large percentage of organic matter. It is loose, fibrous, and well aerated. It does not tend to crust over and crack like heavy clay or fine sandy soil. It absorbs and holds moisture. Soluble fertilizers are stored in it for long periods and losses through leaching are lessened. Nutrients in available form are released slowly and there is less danger of burning through over-fertilization.

The quickest and safest way for most of us to prepare this soil is by composting sod and manure. Commercial florists once followed this method but now find it impractical since their operations have grown so large. Instead, they use soil prepared in the field, as described later.

Composted Sod

Composting is best done during fall or spring when sod is heavy and moist. Select sod with plenty of thick roots. Plan for a pile 5 to 6 feet wide by any reasonable length, depending upon the quantity required—but no higher than 4 to 5 feet. Topsoil from the garden can be used in place of sod, but sod is much better for it adds substance. Stack the sod or topsoil in layers about 8 inches thick and place 4-inch layers of manure in between; use either fresh or rotted cow or horse manure. If manure isn't available, use dehydrated manure in layers about 1½ inches thick. On top of each manure layer spread superphosphate at the rate of about three pounds to every 100 square feet. Some gardeners use a complete fertilizer such as a 5-10-5 instead, but undoubtedly it is better to start young plants in the greenhouse more slowly and to add nitrogen and potash later when the more mature growth can take it. The superphosphate can do no harm even in larger quantities for it is available slowly.

Keep the top of the pile depressed in the center to let rain water run in rather than off. Additional water should not be needed during spring or fall, but if the weather should be dry, wet down the pile with a hose, for moisture is necessary to decomposition.

Grass clippings, and other vegetative matter that decomposes rapidly, may also be added to the pile. Leaves and coarse materials, which take a year or more to decompose, are best left out. Use these in your regular compost heap. *Do not* include disease- or insect-infested matter unless you are sure your pile will generate a temperature of about 150° while decomposing. A pile containing one-third part of fresh manure will reach that temperature. The heat should be sufficient to destroy most insects and disease spores.

The stack should be turned with a fork after six weeks so the material on top and outside will become completely decomposed, too. In another six weeks, the soil will be ready.

When taking soil for use, slice it downward from top to bottom with a spade. Then run it through a half-inch-mesh screen. Since the soil is naturally loose and friable, it should be fine enough for most purposes after being put through a ½-inch sieve. Additional sieving through a ¼-inch-mesh screen will be necessary for planting seed and potting young plants. Too much sieving, however, tends to make soil powdery and fine so it will compress under numerous waterings.

Florists prepare soil in the field by growing and plowing in green cover crops such as rye, cow peas, buckwheat, or soybeans. After decomposition, the soil is ready to use, but addition of peat moss or leaf mold, up to about one-third, is necessary, especially with clay loam. Superphosphate is added at the rate of three pounds to every 100 square feet, for most soils are deficient in phosphorous.

The Compost Heap

Compost made from rotted leaves and vegetable matter is also useful in the greenhouse, but it takes longer to prepare than a sod pile. If you have the space available you should have both. The heap can be kept out of sight in a bin, and both it and the composted sod pile are easily concealed from view with a trellis or shrubbery. Everything can go into the compost heap: leaves, straw, grass clippings, weeds, vegetation from the garden, old bulbs, also manure, if you have it. The heap should be kept moist and piled in saucer-shape so that the moisture will stay in the center. In dry, hot weather, a covering of boards, burlap, tarpaulin, or whatever you have, helps to hold in moisture. A mixture, by weight, consisting of 45 parts ammonium sulfate, 15 parts superphosphate and 40 parts ground limestone greatly aids decomposition. One hundred and fifty pounds of this mixture is recommended per ton of compost; * use less if the material is very wet. The pile should be turned over about every four months.

Compost is usually very light and can be mixed with a generous quantity of garden loam. If it is to be sterilized, the additional soil should be added first.

Soil Sterilization

Sterilization of soil is good practice, but not always essential. There are probably more greenhouse crops grown in untreated soil than in treated soil. Soil sterilization is easily accomplished today, and the odds are on the side of plants grown in it.

Commercial growers operating on a large scale use steam sterilization. By this method steam under pressure, is forced through the soil for half an hour by means of perforated or porous tile pipe until the soil reaches a temperature of 180 to 200°. Equipment involved makes this impractical for amateurs, even on a small scale, but there are several preparations on the market that can be used instead, and they are not difficult or dangerous.

For larger quantities of soil, I like to use one of the gas-forming preparations such as Dow-Fume MC-2, or Larvacide, which do a real job of sterilizing. Both are dangerous poisons but don't let that scare you. Anyone with a little common horse-sense can use them without fear. These preparations are available with complete di-

* A ton of compost is approximately 25 to 30 cu. ft.

rections and convenient in size for home greenhouse gardeners. And the big things sterilization does for your soil makes their use very worth while:

1. Weed seeds are killed—a tremendous help when you have planted slow-germinating seed.
2. Fungus spores and nematodes are controlled.
3. Soil insects are eliminated.

One drawback is that sterilizing must be done when the soil temperature is 50 to 60° or higher. Treatment at lower temperatures is not practical. This means most of us can use these preparations only in summer, unless we have a warm shed or empty greenhouse available at other times. Manure, peat moss, leaf mold, or whatever you add to your soil, should be put in before sterilization. Tools, pots, and seed flats can easily be treated at the same time.

Feeding

When soil is properly prepared to start with, additional fertilizer will not be needed at first. New soils have enough stored nutrients for several weeks' growth, especially when plants are small. A feeding can be given about every two weeks while plants are forming buds. Fertilizer should be given sparingly at first, and never during dull cloudy periods, when growth is slow. At such times it is a poison instead of a benefit. To apply fertilizer at the wrong time is like forcing an invalid to eat a hearty meal. On the other hand, plants should never want for nourishment.

Liquid Fertilizer

Liquid fertilizer is a favorite for use during winter. Not only can it be distributed more evenly than dry, but nutrients are quickly available to plants. There is also less waste. You fertilize and water in one operation, thus saving time. The undesirable residues, which often accumulate in soil when dry fertilizers are used, tend to be eliminated since 90 per cent of the nitrogen, all of the potassium, and about 40 per cent of the phosphorous go into solution.

There are many good complete liquid fertilizers on the market which contain all the minor or trace elements as well as the primary nutrients. In most sections of the country, these trace elements are already present in soil. You probably know whether or not your soil contains them in sufficient quantity. If you're not sure, use one of the complete preparations, for it is advisable to use just a *little more* fertilizer than necessary under glass as any excess is quickly leached out. I have found that cacti, succulents, and plants of the gesneria family—African violets, streptocarpus, and gloxinias—respond particularly well to these complete liquid fertilizers.

If you wish to make up your own liquid fertilizer at a fraction of the cost of commercial preparations, here's a formula that has been recommended by Dr. O. W. Davidson of Rutgers University: 9 pounds ammonium phosphate; 6 pounds ammonium sulfate; and 4½ pounds either muriate of potash, potassium chloride, or potassium sulfate.

Make a stock solution by mixing these ingredients in 5 gallons of water. Before using, dilute at the rate of 4 per cent or 10 tablespoonsful to a gallon of water. Use the diluted solution on bench crops at the rate of one quart to each square foot of space. This is equal to two-and-one-half pounds of dry fertilizer to 10 square feet. For pot plants, a cupful of diluted solution to a 4-inch pot or two cups to a 6-inch pot is about right. Older plants crowded with roots will require more.

Nitrogen is the greatest factor in boosting plant growth. It is especially noticeable in color and growth rate of foliage. A deficiency of nitrogen is evident when growth is stunted and there is an even yellowing of all leaves. Supplying the right amount of nitrogen is important, because an overdose weakens resistance to disease, develops succulent growth, makes stems limp, and retards maturity. Ammonium sulfate, ammonium chloride, and nitrate of soda are good sources of quickly available nitrogen. Ammonium sulfate and nitrate of soda should be mixed at the proportion of one level tablespoon to a gallon of water; ammonium chloride at one teaspoon to a gallon of water.

Phosphorous stimulates root growth and hastens maturity. It improves the condition of soil and balances the effect of nitrogen. Plants can take a lot of phosphorous, and require more than is ordinarily present in the soil. Superphosphate is one of the best fertilizers for supplying phosphorous quickly. When phosphorous is lacking, yellowing along the edges of leaves and a dropping of foliage is noticeable. Good sources of phosphorous are listed later.

Potash puts strength into plants and improves the quality of foliage, flowers, and fruit. It gives firmness to growth, and good green color to foliage. It also increases resistance to disease. That's why you'll hear old gardeners call wood ashes from the fireplace "powdered sunshine."

When soil is deficient in potash, leaves become speckled and brown on the edges. Muriate of potash and potassium chloride mixed one tablespoon to a gallon of water may be used, if wood ashes are not available.

Re-Using Old Soil

Soils that have been used before should be supplied with fertilizers to make up for that leached away through frequent watering, or taken out by the plants. General recommendations call for the addition of a complete fertilizer, such as 4-12-4 or 5-10-5, and superphosphate at the rate of two pounds of the former and three pounds of the latter per 100 square feet of bench area. They should be thoroughly mixed into the soil.

When first applied, the reaction to artificial fertilizers is slowly noticeable. In fact, it is almost unnoticeable, if the soil contains a large amount of manure. It is when the soil becomes almost fully depleted of its nutrients that reactions become apparent.

Leaching to Remove Excess Salts From the Soil: When greenhouse soils have been heavily fertilized over a long period of time, insoluble salts accumulate to such an extent that the roots cannot assimilate nourishment. This excess can be removed by two or three good applications of water. The water is applied at half-hour intervals in sufficient quantity to flow through the soil and out the drainage cracks in the bench.

Dry Commercial Fertilizers

I once heard a fertilizer manufacturer say, "I wouldn't give two cents for a fertilizer that didn't smell." By that he meant that the product should contain matter that decomposes readily and becomes quickly available. In the greenhouse connected with a home, dry fertilizers or nutrient solutions made from salts are likely to be more popular.

It is not necessary to have a large assortment of fertilizers for the greenhouse. A good booster such as described above, and one or two others to supply the potassium and potash should be sufficient, along with lime and peat, to condition the soil. The following is most generally used for the greenhouse.

Complete fertilizers, such as 4-12-4 or 5-10-5 are frequently used as a top dressing, as well as for mixing with the soil at the time of planting. The quantity may range from a small pinch for a small plant up to a teaspoonful for a husky plant. For general application, it is spread at the rate of about two pounds per 100 square feet of bench area. The fertilizer is worked into the surface of the soil lightly. Immediately after application, the soil should be watered. When mixing with new soil, apply a 3-inch pot to a bushel of soil.

Superphosphate is the quickest source of phosphorous. It is less expensive and better than bone meal, because it contains more available phosphoric acid. However, other salts that may be in the soil influence its availability. Nitrate of soda decreases it, since it raises the pH or makes the soil more alkaline, while ammonium sulfate increases it. This is one of the reasons why it is recommended for greenhouse use. Since phosphorous does not move or penetrate deeply into the soil when used as a top dressing, the superphosphate should be mixed with the soil before planting, at the rate of a 5-inch pot to a bushel of soil.

Bone meal is often used as a source of phosphorous, but it acts too slowly to be of real value. It is perfectly satisfactory to put in the compost heap if applied to stimulate bacterial action six months or more before the soil is to be used, but superphosphate is a much less expensive means of putting quickly available phosphorous in the soil. Apply bone meal at the rate of five pounds per 100 square feet.

Wood ashes, if not permitted to lie out of doors where they will become leached out, are a good source of potash. Apply four to six pounds per 100 square feet of soil, or a 4- to 6-inch potful to the bushel.

Muriate of potash is another good source of potassium. Apply a 2-inch potful to a bushel of soil.

Horn shavings are used principally to mix with potting soil. Many old timers swear by them. They are high in phosphorous, but more expensive than most fertilizers. Use a 4-inch potful to a bushel of soil.

Dried blood contains a high percentage of quickly available nitrogen. Mix it with soil at the rate of a 2-inch potful to the bushel, or two to three pounds per 100 square feet.

Lime is a soil corrective and conditioner. It may be used to raise the (pH) alkalinity of acid soils to a point where the nutrients are more available, and to break down the particles of clay soil to make it more friable. Hydrated lime or ground limestone may be used. Ground limestone is preferred because its action is slower and not so destructive to the humus in the soil. Twenty-five percent more limestone is required to produce the equivalent action of a given quantity of hydrated lime. Hydrated lime is used at the rate of a 3-inch to 4-inch potful to a bushel of soil, or four to five pounds per 100 square feet.

Peat moss is another soil conditioner and is mixed with soil to make up for a deficiency of humus. It is sterile, spongy and holds a large quantity of water, which causes the soil to retain moisture. While it helps make the soil more airy and is full of organic matter, it contains very little plant food and is acid in reaction, but this is not important. It is mixed with soil up to one-third by volume.

Leaf mold may be used in place of, or with, peat moss for lightening soil and adding humus. It is widely used in making up potting soil. Like peat moss, it does not have much substance by itself to make plant growth. Mix with soil up to one-third by volume.

Soil conditioners such as Krilium are a tremendous aid in increasing drainage. Mix them with soil at the rate of two tablespoons to the cubic foot but do not use soil for forty-eight hours afterward.

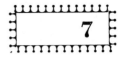

7

Plants for Cut Flowers

The plants in this chapter are best suited to bench culture for cut flowers throughout the winter. Some are also excellent as potted plants.

Aster—CALLISTEPHUS CHINENSIS

The usual difficulties experienced with asters out of doors are easily overcome in the greenhouse. Insect and disease troubles, especially "the yellows" which is spread by leafhoppers, can be controlled effectively. Wire or cheesecloth screens over ventilators are all you need to eliminate these disease-bearing pests.

Seed sown in February provides bloom by June and July, but a May sowing grows faster and is a spectacular sight in August when the greenhouse ordinarily is not in full use. Of course, with additional light a crop is possible during any season. Forty-watt fluorescent lights 2 feet above the plants for four hours a day are adequate. More light induces delicate stem growth. For January bloom, sow seed in July, bench plants in August, and give additional light from September on.

Asters thrive in the same medium-textured, fertile soil suitable for other cut flowers, but never use the same soil for a second aster crop. The trouble-making germs that cause stem-rot live on and continue to cause trouble. Set plants about 12 inches apart, and keep growth stripped of all but six to eight of the huskiest branches.

Continuous, unrestricted root growth is the big thing with asters. Never let them become pot-bound or suffer a setback for want of water or nutrients. Once growth hardens and development is checked, the plants may as well be thrown on the trash heap, for they will never recover.

Always use wilt-resistant aster strains from the best greenhouse seed suppliers. There are single- and double-flowered forms in beautiful colors. With the exception of chrysanthemums, no other plant can equal asters, for cut flowers.

Babys-Breath—GYPSOPHILA ELEGANS

It's a good idea to have babys-breath on hand at all times for use as a filler for bouquets. It is easily flowered in shallow benches or seed flats. Starting in December, make successive sowings every few weeks in light, well-drained soil. Space rows 6 inches apart and thin out seedlings to 3 inches apart within rows. Grow at 45 to 50°.

This is another plant that can be flowered earlier with additional light. The small-flowered varieties like Paris Market last the longest. G. e. carminea is a good red.

Blue Lace-Flower—TRACHYMENE CAERULEA
(Didiscus caerulea)

This lovely plant makes a pleasing addition to mixed bouquets and provides blue flowers when this color is scarce. Seeds sown in December flower during April and

May. A June sowing can be flowered in November and December.

Grow at a 50° temperature in light, fertile soil. Care is required in watering to avoid stunted growth.

Calendula—CALENDULA OFFICINALIS

The calendula is popular in the greenhouse because its large showy flowers can be had from October through June with very little effort or attention. Three plantings are necessary: one in late July for flowers from October through January; a second about the middle of October for bloom from February to March, and a third in November for flowers from April through June.

Colors range from light lemon to rich orange. Ball's Improved varieties are considered best. Lemon Queen is bright yellow; Apricot, brown-yellow; Masterpiece, deep orange.

The plants are benched about 10 inches apart in soil 5 to 6 inches deep. If all but six to eight buds are picked off, the flowers will be larger with longer stems. A cool night temperature, 45 or even 40°, especially during dull fall and winter days, is the secret to the finest blooms. Higher temperatures produce soft, weak growth and small flowers.

Carnation—DIANTHUS CARYOPHYLLUS

The perpetual-flowering carnations of the florist trade provide fragrant blooms in beautiful colors all year. The flowers are lasting and have many uses, but it takes about a hundred plants for a good supply.

When you buy young plants be sure they come from reliable sources, for only clean, healthy growth yields well. Propagation is from cuttings any time from December through February. Side shoots, with or without a heel, root in about three weeks. Transplant these into pots or plant bands and then into benches before they become pot-bound. About May 15th the plants may be set out in the garden for the summer, if this is more convenient, but they are easier to keep healthy in the greenhouse.

In the greenhouse, bench plants about 6 inches apart and no deeper than they previously grew. Pinch to induce side branches until the middle of September. Plants grown in the garden all summer are moved into the greenhouse during August.

Never let plants suffer for lack of food. They are heavy feeders and draw continually on soil nutrients. Feed three or four times with liquid fertilizer from summer through fall, and start feeding again in February if the weather is bright. Good ventilation and an even, cool temperature of 48 to 50° is a must with carnations, so be sure to leave the roof ventilators open an inch or two at night when the outside temperature is above 38°.

Only one flower bud is allowed to develop to a stem, all others must be rubbed off as soon as they appear. Use good supports to keep the plants erect. Wiring-frames of galvanized pipe from which wire may be stretched in tiers between rows, or one of the patented galvanized-wire carnation supports should be provided as soon as plants are benched.

Cornflower— CENTAUREA CYANUS

This is the most popular flower for men's buttonholes—the only one that most men will wear—so it's always good to have some handy in the greenhouse. The many long-stemmed varieties now available also go well in a mixed bouquet. Large-flowered plants from seeds sown in January mature in May. Set plants in benches about 6 inches apart, and pinch back to encourage branching.

Flowers in February are possible with additional light. For this crop, seeds are sown in September. Use 40-watt lamps spaced 4 feet apart, and turn on for four hours a night for sixty days after benching. Grow at 50°.

Improved strains include Blue Boy, Black Boy, Pinkie, Red Boy, and Snowman. Jubilee Gem, a dwarf, makes a good pot plant.

C. imperialis and C. americana are also suited for forcing but must be kept on the dry side.

Chrysanthemum (Annual)—CHRYSANTHEMUM CARINATUM

These spring-blooming daisy-type flowers are easily raised from seed and make a good crop to follow fall chrysanthemums. A September sowing produces plants ready to bench in late December. Place plants about 7 inches apart. Pinch to cause branching and to produce many more flowers.

Wiring-frames are required for support. The flowering period is April, but early blooms may be had with artificial light, as with cornflowers.

Eldorado and Northern Star are good greenhouse varieties. Mixtures of bright strains are also popular.

Chrysanthemum—CHRYSANTHEMUM MORIFOLIUM

You will make no mistake if you fill nearly every foot of your greenhouse with chrysanthemums each fall. Nothing you can grow is quite so handsome and satisfying. They occupy your greenhouse only a short time and their requirements are simple from start to finish. You can have them for cutting by the basketful in numerous types, sizes, colors, and forms, from small bunches of buttons to huge single-stemmed standards.

Use loose fibrous soil from your composted sod pile and grow the plants in benches or pots. Fertilizing is not necessary in the beginning if the soil is good to start with, but plants should be watered with liquid fertilizer every two weeks from the time buds set until they show color.

Plants thrive if mulched with peat moss during summer; 60 to 65° is needed for bud formation but thereafter grow plants at 50°.

Distance between plants in benches depends upon the variety. A free circulation of air around them is essential for healthy growth. You will probably buy rooted cuttings the first year at least, and dealers' catalogs will furnish directions for planting distances, pinching, and disbudding of varieties you select.

Pinching will induce three or four branches to develop. The first pinch should be taken about twenty-five days after planting. Timed pinching is most important to the development of sprays. If pinched too early, the crown bud is too low and underdeveloped. Late pinching reduces the number of flowers per stem. The usual practice is to allow three or four stems to develop to each plant except in the case of disbuds on which four to six stems may be left.

Plants grown with a single flower to a stem are pinched only once. This is done to eliminate the crown bud, when the terminal bud is selected for the flower. It is distinguished from the others by many smaller buds surrounding it. These are rubbed off when large enough. Of course, all side and basal shoots at the axils of leaves must be religiously removed as soon as they appear.

Should no crown bud appear, one of the strongest and

straightest surrounding shoots is permitted to grow. The stem will be crooked but this cannot be helped.

Chrysanthemums should not be grown cool, although they once were considered a cool plant. They form their buds from the 15th to the 20th of August, some as late as the 25th when the temperature is 55° or higher. If the temperature is lower at this season, blindness results. Be sure to keep the temperature up to 55° and never let it become lower than 40°. This is particularly important with varieties that flower late in houses that are inclined to run on the cool side.

Remember to keep the chrysanthemums well watered. Give them a good watering when they are first set in the bench. Later in the year, the amount of water can be reduced, for the foliage on plants will shade the soil and reduce evaporation. Mulching is especially beneficial. Peat moss makes one of the best mulches since it contains a large amount of nitrogen.

Before plants have started to make considerable growth in the benches, a means of supporting them should be provided. Bench wiring-frames, with wire running lengthwise along the bench and strings across, are best. Heavy wire stakes with several Twist-ems or strings to hold the stem straight are satisfactory. In tying stems, care should be taken to make a loose loop to permit further growth.

The usual flowering period for chrysanthemums is from October to January, but you can have them all year by shading and by supplying additional light. Dealers' catalogs give directions according to variety.

Propagation. When plants have finished flowering, the best are selected as stock plants to provide cuttings for the following season. These are cut back and stored in new soil in pots, deep flats, or benches, out in direct sunlight. Since plants are dormant, they should be kept in a cool place in the greenhouse with soil on the dry side, but they must have sun, ample space, and adequate attention to keep them free of insects, just like your finest actively growing plants.

Cuttings may be taken in April for early varieties, through May for midseason varieties, and in June for late varieties. Select only strong, healthy stock with close joints. Cuttings from 3 to 5 inches long are made with a slanting cut below a joint. These are rooted in sand, a sand and peat-moss mixture, or vermiculite. Rooting takes place in three weeks. Transplant immediately into 3-inch pots or plant bands. Never permit cuttings to remain too long in the propagating bench, or they will become stunted and worthless.

Potted plants will require periodical shifting so they do not become pot-bound and stunted. Plants can be grown attractively in 5- to 8-inch pots.

When it comes to varieties suitable for growing in a small- to moderate-size greenhouse, Fred Lindeman of the National Chrysanthemum Society, and a winner of many awards, offers these suggestions:

SPRAY TYPES

NAME	COLOR	TYPE	FLOWERING DATE
Bright Forecast	Yellow	Button Pompon	Oct. 10th
Polaris	Daisy	Medium Single	Oct. 5th
Emerel	Chinese Yellow	Medium Decorative	Oct. 10th
Gold Coast	Lemon Yellow	Medium Pompon	Oct. 25th
Arcadia	White	Medium Pompon	Oct. 28th
Treasure	Yellow	Small Pompon	Oct. 10th
Dwight Douglass	Golden Yellow	Large Decorative	Oct. 5th
Charles Nye	Yellow	Medium Decorative	Oct. 5th
Yellow Chris. Columbus	Yellow	Medium Decorative	Oct. 1st

NAME	COLOR	TYPE	FLOWERING DATE
Classic	White	Semiformal Pompon	Oct. 10th
Silver Plate	White	Medium Decorative	Oct. 12th
Christopher Columbus	White	Medium Decorative	Oct. 1st
Popcorn	White	Medium Pompon	Oct. 25th
Limelight	White	Pompon	Oct. 5th
Maestro	White	Medium Pompon	Oct. 10th
Norona	White	Button Pompon	Oct. 15th
White Doty	Ivory White	Large Pompon	Nov. 1st
Carolyn Yosick	Lavender	Medium Pompon	Oct. 20th
Pink Dot	Light Pink	Medium Pompon	Oct. 25th
Masquerade	Lavender Rose	Pompon	Oct. 10th
Royal Robe	Purple	Decorative	Sept. 15th
Enterprise	Amaranth	Medium Pompon	Oct. 15th
Edith Roberts	Light orchid pink	Small Pompon	Oct. 25th
Carnival	Burnt orange	Large Pompon	Oct. 10th
Bonfire	Bright red	Decorative	Oct. 1st
Avalon	Orange bronze	Pompon	Oct. 5th
Mona	Rust bronze	Pompon	Oct. 5th
Marionette	Rust red	Pompon	Sept. 25th
Miguel	Raspberry red	Decorative	Oct. 8th
Success	Deep crimson	Large Decorative	Oct. 8th
Red Velvet	Dark crimson	Large Decorative	Oct. 5th
Admiral	Dark red	Decorative	Oct. 12th
Blue Blood	Amaranth red	Decorative	Oct. 10th

LARGE FLOWERING DISBUDS

NAME	COLOR	TYPE	FLOWERING DATE
Celestra	Lemon yellow	Semi-incurved	Oct. 20th
Citrus Queen	Pure yellow	Anemone	Nov. 10th
Yellow Lace	Pure yellow	Spider type	Oct. 25th
Lorraine	Clearest yellow	Spider type	Nov. 5th
Oriole	Golden yellow	Large incurved	Nov. 1st
Watanabe	Light yellow	Large incurved	Oct. 15th
Blazing Gold	Golden yellow	Medium incurved	Oct. 15th
Elegence	White	Large exhibition	Nov. 5th
White Frieda	White yellow	Cushion anemone	Nov. 5th
Sterling	White	Large incurved	Nov. 10th
Albatross	White	Large incurved	Nov. 1st
Queen's Lace	White	Quilled spider	Oct. 25th
White Supreme	White	Incurved spider	Nov. 1st
White Frill	White	Exceptionally long frilly petals	Oct. 25th
Gaiety	Rich wine red	Giant incurved	Oct. 20th
Bess Witt	Apricot bronze and salmon pink	Quilled	Oct. 20th

NAME	COLOR	TYPE	FLOWERING DATE
Serene	Coppery bronze	Spider	Nov. 1st
Rhythm	Buff bronze	Spider	Nov. 5th
Muto's Crimson	Deep maroon with gold	Reverse	Nov. 5th
Ben Leighton	Wine red	Large incurved	Oct. 20th
Doris Louise	Pink yellow	Cushion anemone	Nov. 5th
Autumn Queen	Soft pink	Large incurved	Nov. 1st
Bunbu	Orchid pink	Frilled spider	Oct. 25th
Pink Chief	Orchid pink	Large incurved	Oct. 20th

Clarkia—CLARKIA ELEGANS

Under glass, clarkia grows 3 or 4 feet tall, with graceful sprays of rose-tinted flowers. Sow seeds in January for May flowering. Transplant seedlings into flats about 3 inches apart and later bench about 8 inches apart. Grow in poor soil at a 50° temperature and keep plants on the dry side. Trim off side branches for development of long sprays. Try Orange King, Salmon Queen, White King, and Brilliant King. With additional light, flowering is possible in February.

Feverfew—MATRICARIA CAPENSIS

Here's another easy-to-grow white flower for background bouquet material. Plants from seed sown in October, or cuttings rooted in December, ordinarily bloom by May, but six weeks or more may be gained with artificial light used from December on. Grow at a temperature of 50°. Ball's Double White provided one hundred per cent double flowers for me.

Larkspur—DELPHINIUM AJACIS

This is a splendid crop to follow late chrysanthemums. Long, graceful sprays in white, lilac, rose, blue, and salmon, will be ready to cut in April from a December sowing. Plants should be ready for 3-inch pots or plant bands during January and for benching in February. Set 10 inches apart in light soil and grow at 45 to 50°. The Supreme varieties are popular.

Lupine—LUPINUS HARTWEGII

The annual lupine makes a good crop for spring. An August sowing flowers during March, and another made in January will be ready by May. Start seeds in 3-inch pots. When plants are large enough, set them 12 inches apart in benches. Side branches flower after the first spike blooms, but stems are shorter and often crooked.

Marguerites—CHRYSANTHEMUM FRUTESCENS

It may be that I am especially partial to daisy-type blooms, but I find many others are, too. Perhaps it is because they yield such an abundance of flowers over so long a period. You can grow marguerites in benches or pots, but bench-grown plants are larger, have better foliage, and longer-stemmed flowers. About four or five plants are enough in a small greenhouse.

Cuttings rooted in August or September will be ready to bench in November. If you don't have stock plants, buy a few small potted cuttings from a florist. They will start blooming by March, and continue into June. Additional light will bring flowers two to three weeks earlier. Pinch to make plants full and bushy. Stock plants can be carried through the summer in the garden.

Boston Yellow Daisy is one of the best yellows. It is exceptionally long-lasting as a cut flower. Mrs. F. Sanders is an excellent white both indoors and out. Nicholson's Giant White Marguerite is another good variety.

Marigold—TAGETES ERECTA

Start seeds in August to have plants ready to bench by September 15th for December to January bloom. A January sowing will flower in April. Set plants 4 or 5 inches apart and trim off side branches so strength will go into flowers.

Marigolds like a moderate temperature of not less than 55°. Plant only winter-forcing varieties such as, Leib's Brown and Gold; Leib's Winter Sunshine, a golden-yellow; Golden Trumpet, an odorless yellow; Colorado Sunshine, a butter-yellow.

Mignonette—RESEDA ODORATA

Try a few plants of this old-time favorite even though you may not have found it especially attractive in the garden. It is another of those flowers that does so much better under glass.

Seeds are sown in July for winter flowering, and again in January for spring bloom. If long stems are wanted, do not pinch, and remove any single shoots that may occur. Pinch twice for bushy plants and for numerous flowers on 12-inch stems. Grow at 45°.

Nemesia—NEMESIA STRUMOSA

Grow nemesia as a bench crop or showy pot plant. The showy flowers resembling orchids in blue, orange, pink, red, white, and mixed shades have stems 18 inches long when well grown. A November sowing flowers by April, another in January will be ready to cut by May.

Set plants about 8 inches apart in the bench, or grow three to an 8-inch pot. Use a medium-texture soil of low fertility and keep it fairly dry. Pinch once or twice to induce branching. Grow at 50°.

N.s. nana compacta varieties are dwarf, 6 to 8 inches high, and flower well in a bulb pan or seed flat.

Pansy—VIOLA TRICOLOR

Never be without a large quantity of pansy plants for the small greenhouse. They can be counted on for many cheerful blooms in a small amount of space. Grow only the long-stemmed varieties. Seeds are expensive but the outstanding flowers produced are worth it. Large flowers from 3 to 4 inches in diameter with stems as long as 16 inches are easily possible.

Sow seeds carefully in a cold frame during July. Bench 10 to 12 inches apart during October and November in rich light soil, or grow in 6-inch pots.

Pansies are heavy feeders, so for vigorous, healthy growth it is important that soil be good. Add manure and sand, if necessary.

A night temperature of 45° is desirable, but lower or slightly higher temperatures are not harmful. Pick the blooms so they will not go to seed, just as with outdoor-grown plants. Good bedding varieties also flower well in the greenhouse and the colors are more brilliant. Pansies want all possible light and respond well to artificial light.

Painted Tongue—SALPIGLOSSIS SINUATA

You seldom see this plant in greenhouses, although the large flowers in red, blue, yellow, purple, and violet, go very well in bouquets. Sow seeds in January for flowering in May. An October sowing flowers in March when additional light is provided.

Scarlet Sage—SALVIA SPLENDENS

This is another plant that deserves more popularity, for the gay spikes are easily grown. Start plants from cuttings of your outdoor plants in the fall. They will take hold quickly and flower by midwinter. For early spring blooms, start seeds or cuttings in January. Grow at 60°.

Snapdragon—ANTIRRHINUM MAJUS

Many greenhouse gardeners feel that I put too much emphasis on snapdragons but, except for chrysanthemums or asters, no plants are quite so attractive for cut flowers, or so easily grown. With successive sowings you can have them any month of the year. Nothing ever happens to them, either. Plants are rugged and can even take light freezing for short periods. They make good growth in any medium- to heavy-textured soil and do not need fertilizer until well established. They are then fed with a complete liquid fertilizer every three to four weeks.

Sow seed thinly in a bulb pan and as soon as plants are large enough to handle, transfer to 3-inch pots or other flats. Do not add fertilizer to the soil or growth will become grassy.

Unpinched plants grown to a single stem bloom earlier and may be set closer together—3 inches apart in summer, or 4 inches in winter. After the first flowers are cut, side branches will produce bloom, and although stems of the second cutting will be shorter, you have flowers over a longer period. Plants of a pinched crop are set 6 by 8 inches apart. Make the first pinch when five or six leaves have appeared. Plants with five or six branches yield well.

Seeds sown about the middle of July produce a crop

that can be benched after chrysanthemums are finished, using the same soil. They will flower from late December through March. A crop started in October will yield in late February or early March. For a May to June crop, sow seeds in January.

Plants should be supported to keep stems straight and to give the greenhouse a professional appearance. Bench wiring-frames, stakes, or specially made wire loops, which can be bought from seedsmen, may be used. The plants want a night temperature ranging from 45 to 50°, with about ten to fifteen degrees higher during the day. High temperatures produce soft growth which does not flower well. The seeds of good greenhouse varieties are expensive but worth the price. They are produced in greenhouses by specialists, especially for winter flowering.

Stevia—PIQUERIA TRINERVIA

Dainty white, fragrant flowers of the long-stemmed stevia add grace to any bouquet. Cuttings rooted in May can be potted in June and carried in a coldframe through the summer. In October they are benched in the greenhouse where they will flower from December well into February.

Work superphosphate into the soil at the rate of a 4-inch potful to 10 square feet of soil. Grow at 45 to 50°.

Stock—MATHIOLA INCANA

If stock has not flowered well for you out of doors, it is probably because temperatures were too high. Flower buds will not form well at temperatures over 60°, but many are produced in a 45 to 50° greenhouse. Grow either the columnar-type or single-stem plants which grow fast and produce long-stemmed spikes of double flowers or branching-type flowers over a long period of time.

Sow seeds in August for a January crop. With additional light they can be brought into bloom two weeks earlier. Successive sowings for flowers through June should be made every other month up through February.

The flower spikes need support to produce straight stems. Wiring-frames or stakes like those for carnations or snapdragons are used. Select only the best greenhouse varieties.

Sweet Peas—LATHYRUS ODORATUS

Try a few sweet peas even though you may not have room for many. They thrive at 40 to 45° and not only do the fragrant blooms add charm to the greenhouse but they are handy for corsages and bouquets.

Grow plants in raised benches or ground-beds using rich, well-drained soil. The addition of wood ashes at the rate of three pounds to 25 square feet of bench is helpful.

Plants can be started in pots to conserve bench space. Sow three or four seeds to a pot. After these are well rooted, bench them about 3 inches apart in rows 7 inches apart.

Strings or wire held by small stakes at the base of the plant and extending to the roof of the greenhouse are used to support the plant. When growth reaches the glass, the vines are slipped down along the strings so the new growth can continue.

Give sweet peas plenty of moisture in sunny weather, and grow cool—45 to 50° at night. Ventilate well in the daytime; if possible, temperature should not exceed 65°.

November to June is the blooming period for sweet

peas. Seeds sown in August start flowering in November and produce well into March. An October planting blooms from February through May, and one started in November comes into flower during March continuing through May.

Bud drop, which occurs with sweet peas, is caused by sudden dips in temperature, overcrowding of plants, too much soil moisture, and excessive applications of fertilizer in relation to the amount of sunshine.

Winter-flowering varieties are best, except for the late spring crop, when the Cuthbertson strains are better.

Transvaal Daisy—GERBERIA JAMESONII

Good plants of the new large-flowered varieties are inexpensive to buy from specialists and will grow on year after year. Plants grown from seed sown in February, bloom the following year.

Bench plants about 10 inches apart in light soil that is on the alkaline side (pH 7.5). Divide clumps in June and, if more convenient, set them out in the garden until late August. Most growers say a temperature of 55° gives the best bloom, but I have had good luck in a 50° greenhouse. Feed with liquid fertilizer in spring and fall.

Violet—VIOLA ODORATA

So few violets are grown today that it is hard to believe they were once the most popular corsage flower. Good plants yield well from fall to spring and are no trouble to grow in a cool greenhouse. Use any soil, but work in one pound of superphosphate and two pounds of wood ashes to 10 square feet of bench. Buy rooted plants in the fall and set these about 10 inches apart with the crowns well up. Remove any runners and yellow leaves that appear.

Grow at 40 to 50° in a well ventilated greenhouse. Keep soil moderately moist and mulched with rotted manure or peat moss.

8

Flowering Plants in Pots

African Violet—SAINTPAULIA

AFRICAN VIOLETS thrive beautifully in the home greenhouse. They are easy to handle and inexpensive to grow. Propagation as well as culture is simple. You can have hundreds of plants flowering every day of the year in a wide variety of forms and colors. You'll find a continual demand for this excellent plant, so you can readily sell your surplus. It is an excellent way to supplement your income.

A loose. porous soil is conducive to good development of the fine root system. Use equal parts soil, sand, rotted manure, peat moss or leaf mold, and feed with liquid fertilizer every two to three weeks. Do not mix a dry complete fertilizer with the potting soil. Apply it sparingly in the beginning, for strong fertilizers burn the delicate root system. Young plants will grow best with more frequent but dilute applications of liquid fertilizer. A half to three-quarters the usual strength recommended

89

by the manufacturer, every three to four weeks, is just right.

Tests made at Ohio State University have shown that a light intensity of 1100 foot candles is generally ideal for African violets. Shading with three layers of cheesecloth is about right in summer, one layer in winter, and two layers in late spring and fall. In hot climates, if permanent slat-shades are used, a single layer of cheesecloth may need to be placed inside. During the short days of winter, supplementary fluorescent light could be used at night to speed up production. A night temperature between 65 and 70°, with a daytime temperature 10 degrees higher, is ideal. Plants will not prosper at low temperatures.

Flowering plants may be produced in eight to ten months by propagation from leaf cuttings, or in six to seven months from seed. Leaf cuttings are more frequently used, except in creating new varieties. Peat moss and clean, coarse sand is widely used as a rooting medium, but vermiculite, or vermiculite mixed with peat moss and sand, are good too.

Only clean, disease-free leaves should be selected for rooting. Take them with a short stem about ½ inch long. If stems are long, roots form deeply, and it takes a longer time for leaves to appear. Cuttings may be planted close together, but set them firmly in the rooting medium so they will not fall over and touch one another. Root-promoting substances hasten root formation, but even with their aid, it takes ten weeks for shoots to become large enough for transplanting.

Young plants are divided into single crowns and set in 2½-inch pots. Plants with several crowns make a good floral display faster, but the foliage is not as attractive.

Plants may be transferred directly to 4- or 5-inch pots, if care can be used in watering—that is, if they can be kept on the dry side until new roots are well developed in the fresh soil. A safer practice would be to transfer from 2½- to 3-inch pots before the shift to a 4- or 5-inch size.

Use tepid water of at least 65° when watering from above. Cold water causes yellow- or cream-colored spots. Water before noon so that foliage will be dry before night.

Subirrigation in watertight benches is the best practice. See Chapter 20. Always keep plants free of rotted leaves and fallen flowers. Space plants to insure free circulation of air, or they may become leggy and diseased.

Cyclamen mite and nematodes are the most serious pests. It is smart to isolate or discard badly infested plants. Cyclamen mite can be recognized by stunted growth and a whitish coloring on the leaves. Flowers will be malformed, and buds will fail to develop. Treat soil with systox, and spray or dip in malathion or parathion.

Nematode infestation can be recognized by familiar root knots and swellings in the stem. There is no control, so isolate or destroy infected plants. The careful gardener will sterilize all soil with Soilfume-Caps or one of the other more effective means described in Chapter 6. He will then root leaves from clean plants only and permit no suspect plants in his greenhouse. Mealy bug, thrips, and aphids are easily controlled with the malathion-DDT spray.

There are many splendid new varieties, and more are coming out each year. Colors, bloom and foliage characteristics, and growth habit are being improved each year. Excellent selections can be made from catalogs of reliable suppliers, but names of varieties are quite confused. The African Violet Society is making a tremendous effort toward standardization. A membership with this group is well worth while, for their splendid quarterly publication alone.

Ageratum—AGERATUM HOUSTONIANUM

Many greenhouse gardeners won't grow ageratum because of its susceptibility to white fly, but with the newer insecticides, this insect is no longer a problem. Lift plants from the outdoor garden, or take cuttings in fall. For spring bedding-plants, sow seed, or take cuttings in February and March. Pinch to induce branching.

Alyssum—ALYSSUM MARITIMUM

Here's a plant, with a delicate fragrance, that flowers all winter. Along the edge of benches it has a beautiful softening effect, yet does not interfere with other plants. Seeds germinate readily any time of year, and flower in four to eight weeks, depending upon the season.

Azalea

Azaleas are easily forced into bloom from Christmas on, and a few pots of them overflowing with brilliant color will be enjoyable to have. The beginner may find them difficult to propagate, but inexpensive plants for forcing may be obtained from specialists. When they arrive, soak the root ball thoroughly in water and then let it drain. Pot firmly in as small a pot as the root will take, using one-half part each of loam and peat moss. Do not add bone meal or anything that would make the soil alkaline.

A temperature of 60°, starting late in September, is

needed to force plants for Christmas. Order special varieties for this purpose.

For the following year's stock, plants can be set out in the garden in spring, either directly in soil, or in pots plunged to the rim. Give them partial shade, spray periodically for thrips and red spider. A yellowing of leaves often indicates iron deficiency. Watering with one ounce of ferrous sulfate to a gallon of water corrects this condition.

Begonia

The begonia gives us several excellent classes of plants to raise for winter and summer flowering and for attractive foliage throughout the year. No wonder it is now one of the most popular plants. For our purpose in making selections and in growing an assortment of begonias in the small greenhouse, they can be arranged in five general groups: Tuberous-rooted begonias, Christmas begonias, Wax begonias, rex begonias, and miscellaneous Fibrous-rooted types, which are of two kinds—Rhizomatous and Non-rhizomatous. There are tall, medium, and hanging basket types.

The *tuberous-rooted type* is by far the showiest, with flowers as large as 6 inches across. There are singles, doubles, frilled, and camellia-flowered varieties in crimson, red, orange, white, light to dark pink, and yellow. The spectacular beauty of these begonias is rapidly increasing their popularity.

In the greenhouse, flowering starts in late spring and continues throughout summer. Partial shade is essential during the bright days of spring and summer, both in the greenhouse and out of doors. When the weather becomes sufficiently warm, plants may be set out under trees or shrubs, where they brighten the garden with their rich color. Plant them where they will get sunshine in the morning and late afternoon, but shade during the heat of the day. Plants may be bedded or left in the pots and plunged to the rim in soil.

Seed sown in February will provide flowering plants by July. Tubers are started in March. Best results are obtained by laying the tubers in sphagnum moss until roots appear, and then potting them in bulb pans. The soil should be light and fibrous, and the drainage good.

In fall, when the foliage begins to go, plants outdoors can be lifted, and the tubers stored in dry sphagnum moss.

The Christmas Begonia. Dutch and Belgian growers have done wonders with this type. Plants become literally covered with bloom in the greenhouse from November into January. They become a compact mass of flowers, and are much more attractive in color than the ordinary Fibrous-rooted or Wax Begonias.

Raise the plants from leaf cuttings or seeds sown in November and December for bloom the following year, or buy small plants in pots during spring. They should be of 4- or 5-inch size by August to provide good plants by winter. Stem cuttings root easily, but the plants grow tall and leggy, and it is practically impossible to make them develop a good, compact form.

The Wax Begonias (semperflorens), including the types of gracilis offered in seed catalogs, are mainly summer-flowering, though they bloom to some extent at all times of year. In this group are all bedding varieties of tall, medium, and dwarf form. Strong growers in the tall, upright class include Christmas Cheer, Glory of Erfurt, Isle de France, Pink Radio, and Silver Wings. In the intermediate, there are Carmen, Fire Sea, Indian Maid, Masterpiece, and Darling; and in the dwarf, Adeline, Ball's White, Luminosa Compacta, and King of the Reds.

The best plants are raised from seed. Seeds sown in December through January bloom from July on.

The Rex-cultorum are ornamental foliage begonias with decorative metallic-colored leaves, in red, bronze, and greenish silver. They bloom in summer, but like most plants having showy foliage, the flowers do not amount to much. Good, popular varieties include Emperor, Glory of St. Albans, Rajah, and Louise Clossom. Many plants in this group are vigorous growers, and do well as house plants. They are easily propagated from leaf cuttings in a mixture of sand, and peat or leaf mold. Propagation from seed is also easy.

Miscellaneous Fibrous-rooted Types. In this group we can consider all the rest of the begonias, both rhizomatous and non-rhizomatous, for they are nearly all grown under a similar system of culture. Among them are some of the most excellent varieties that flower in winter and spring. In the non-rhizomatous group are President Carnot, manicata, Haageana nitida, rosea gigantea, Sachsen, argenteoguttata, Lady Waterlow, coccinea, and Paul Brunta. In the rhizomatous-rooted, Marian, Feastii and its form Bunchii, ricinifolia, and Heracleifolia. They are propagated by stem or leaf cuttings.

Culture. Begonias are easy to grow from seed, but since seed of all varieties is very fine, it should be sown comparatively thinly. Use a light, porous, sandy soil in a bulb pan, and provide good drainage. Water the soil well before sowing seed, and do not cover with soil. Place the pan in a warm part of the greenhouse—65°, and set a pane of glass over the top. Transplant the seedlings into another bulb pan or flat, as soon as they are big enough for safe handling. Later, when the plants are larger, pot them in 2½- or 3-inch pots.

Stem and leaf cuttings are easy to root, but they do best in a glass-covered propagating bench. Of course, care must be taken with ventilation to prevent stem rot and damp-off. Select mature leaves for leaf cuttings, firm growth for stem cuttings, and always plant them firmly. Leaf cuttings should be in close contact with the propagating medium. Peg them, or place pieces of crock on top to hold them down. Cuttings take about four to five weeks to root and should be left in the propagating bed until strong growth appears. Frequent but light feedings with weak liquid fertilizer are helpful at this stage. Soil for the first potting should be light—either leaf mold or peat moss, mixed with sand, is satisfactory. A coarser mixture may be used when plants are shifted to larger pots—four parts loam and rotted manure, one part leaf mold or peat moss, and one part sand.

In the warm, bright weather of spring and summer, all begonias require partial shade—not complete shade. Sunlight in the morning, and at the end of the day, is beneficial; but during hot midday hours, plants should be well shaded. Many begonia fanciers keep their plants in slat houses during summer. Throughout the short days of winter, begonias need full sunlight and a night temperature of 52 to 58°. Aphids, red spiders, mites, thrips, and mealy bugs are common enemies.

Bouvardia—BOUVARDIA HUMBOLDTII *and* B. TERNIFOLIA

This flowering plant has so many uses; you will always want a few on hand. The fragrant bloom clusters not only go well in corsages and bouquets but are a joy in the greenhouse.

Plants are easily perpetuated year after year from cuttings. B. Humboldtii is reproduced from stem cuttings in the usual way, and B. ternifolia from root cuttings taken about 2 inches long and set in sand with one end slightly protruding.

Plants do well in a rich, loose soil and must be kept growing. Once they become hard and pot-bound, they never flower well. Pinch until September, when flower buds form for November and December blooms. Cut back after flowering, and keep on the dry side until February. Then water moderately in preparation for a new batch of cuttings.

Browallia—BROWALLIA SPECIOSA

Blue, purple, or white browallia, in baskets hanging from the rafters, lend a magnificent touch to the greenhouse. Grow this from seed in July or August, transplanting seedlings about 2 inches apart in a sphagnum-moss-lined basket of the size you wish. Browallia also makes an excellent pot plant. Grow at 50 to 55°.

Calceolaria—CALCEOLARIA CRENATIFLORA

In spite of all you hear, calceolaria is not hard to grow if you follow a few simple requirements. In August, start seed in loose sterilized soil at 60°. The seed is fine so press it into the surface, but do not cover. Transplant as soon as seedlings are large enough to handle, and grow cool (50°). Spray or fumigate once a week or aphids will take over. Shade from late February on, and water moderately.

Those dwarf varieties with extra-large flower heads are

best suited to the home greenhouse. Some bloom for a month or more. You can choose solid or spotted colors in red, orange, and yellow.

Cineraria—SENECIO CRUENTUS

Cineraria is a popular greenhouse pot plant because it may be brought into flower from December on by successive sowings. It is brilliantly colored with more than a hundred small blooms to a plant. Sow seeds from May until August, and transplant into flats when ready; then pot in 3-inch pots. Soil should be light, about a quarter sharp sand. Shift into larger pots, as required, adding a 4-inch pot of 4-12-4 fertilizer to a wheelbarrow of soil. Apply a complete liquid fertilizer about once a week. Keep plants growing right along up to 6- or 8-inch bulb pans, if possible. Keep the soil moderately moist, and grow cool—45 to 50°.

Colors range from blue to purple, pink to red, and white. Multiflora nana is very dwarf; grandiflora, Cremer's Prize strain, Multiflora, Grandiflora Marima, Siter's Rainbow strain, and Howard & Smith's strain are large.

Cyclamen

White, pink, and red flowers of cyclamen keep coming for a long period from fall on. The blooms are brilliant against the ruddy, dark green foliage—a great treat for Christmas. The best plants are grown from seed, but cuttings take hold readily in sand during spring or summer. They are made by slicing the corm of an old plant into sections, each with at least one leaf.

For the small greenhouse, it may be more practical to buy young plants from garden suppliers in late August and finish them off. Small plants are inexpensive and quickly make a good show. Seeds are sown from August to December. A cool basement is a good place to start seeds. Germination, which takes about five weeks, is best at 50°.

Set the seedlings in 3-inch pots with a liberal proportion of gravel in the bottom, for they must have good drainage. Soil should be light, and the corm of the plant should be set so that the top is level with the soil. Plants must not become pot-bound or checked, but should be kept growing all the time and transferred into 5- or 6-inch pots when ready. A complete fertilizer, such as 4-12-4, should be added to the soil when shifting.

Keep plants as cool as possible during summer, and place in partial shade. Frequent syringing of the foliage is necessary. In fall, shading should be removed and plants grown at a 50° night temperature. The first flowers are best removed to give strength to the roots. Plants may be carried over for the following year, by withholding water almost entirely after flowering and giving them a rest.

Flowering Maple—ABUTILON

Attractive foliage and drooping pink to red bell-shaped flowers of flowering maple make it desirable as a pot plant in winter; and it can be used for borders of flower beds, or to grow in boxes, in spring.

Propagate from cuttings in fall for winter flowering, and in February for outdoor flower beds. Of course, the growth of plants that have been out in the garden all summer will be too hard to produce good cuttings. Cut growth back and use the newer shoots that soon will appear in quantity. Seed sown in spring produces the best plants for winter flowering. Pinch to make full, shapely plants.

Fuchsia

There is a great variety of fuchsias to grow in tall, short, and trailing forms. The new hybrids are so attractive it is easy to understand why collections are becoming popular.

Plants are propagated by cuttings rooted from August to March. Suckers, about 2 inches long, from the base of the plant are easiest to root. Grow them in coarse soil consisting of loose loam and one-quarter part sharp sand. The plants are heavy feeders and respond well to applications of liquid fertilizer in spring and summer. Grow at a temperature of 50°, and place close to the glass.

Fuchsias flower most freely in spring, but continue intermittently throughout the year. In fall, they become dormant and require potting. The old soil should be replaced with new, but the plants can go back into the same size pot until growth starts. Then shift into larger pots. It takes two years or more to grow those large, showy specimens, and tall standards.

Geraniums

It is good to see geraniums coming into their own. Too many gardeners unknowingly pass "those weeds" by, without realizing the fun and charm of a choice collection. Specialists offer hundreds of varieties that are fascinating in leaf pattern, form, scent, and flower. You will find many outstanding amateur collections, too. Some of my friends have up to three hundred different kinds. There are good books on the subject. "Geraniums—Pelargoniums" by Helen Van Pelt Wilson is a splendid one that makes interesting and informative reading.

Don't overlook the large-flowered geranium of the florist trade, either. It is so easy to raise in quantity for your flower beds, urns, and boxes. You can root the cuttings right in small pots. The percentage that take root may not be so high as those started in a propagating bench, but the time and effort saved makes up for those lost. Root the cuttings in any season you like, but take them by late August for good-size flowering plants by spring. Your outdoor garden plants will provide good cutting-stock before cool weather hardens them off.

Cuttings should be 4 to 5 inches long with two or more leaf buds. Pinch the newly rooted plants several times to get that well-branched, stocky growth with numerous blooms.

When transplanting to 4-inch pots, add a 4-inch potful of superphosphate to each wheelbarrow of soil. Go easy with fertilizers that are high in nitrogen. They make growth too succulent. Keep plants on the dry side in winter, and avoid leaf spot by keeping the foliage dry.

Standards are made by letting the main stem grow unpinched and removing all side growth as soon as it appears. When 3 or 4 feet high, the center is pinched out to make a well-formed head.

Gloxinia—SINNINGIA SPECIOSA

You can grow gloxinias from tubers started in February or March, but the best plants come from seed. Raise them yourself or buy from specialists. This African violet companion should be more widely grown. Good hybrids are inexpensive.

A January sowing will make 5-inch flowering plants

by June. Start them at 70°, pressing the fine seeds into the soil, but do not cover them. Use one-third each of peat moss, loam, and sharp sand. Shade lightly and keep plants growing all the time.

Space young plants 3 inches apart in seed flats or beds for easy handling before potting. Water moderately and with care, never letting the soil dry out. When plants are going good, plant directly in 4-inch pots. Grow at 55 to 60°.

After flowering, plants can be stored in a temperature of 50° and watered just enough to prevent tubers from shriveling. Tubers can also be stored in peat moss. When their dormancy is over and signs of growth begin to appear, they should be repotted with new soil in the same size pot. The old soil is easily removed with water from a hose.

Gloxinias are one of the most striking greenhouse pot plants. Colors are rich, in a wide range of shades from blue to deep purple, pink to red, and white. Frequently the blossoms are edged or streaked with white, making a conspicuous contrast.

Hydrangea—HYDRANGEA MACROPHYLLA

While it is easy to propagate hydrangeas from cuttings in spring or fall, it is far better to buy plants of choice varieties in 5-, 6-, or 7-inch pots available in fall. They can be forced into flower at any temperature from 45 to 65° but, of course, they will flower much earlier in the warmer greenhouse. It takes about six to eight weeks after buds have formed in a temperature of 50 to 60°.

The plants require hardening off before forcing, and may be placed in a deep coldframe from about December 15th up to January 1st, or until wanted. They can stand a temperature as low as 20°. The frame should be covered to keep them in darkness, and since the soil should be moderately moist, pots can be sunk up to the rim in cinders or soil. When the plants are brought into the greenhouse, it is best to place them so that the rise in temperature will be gradual before bringing them out into full sunlight.

Hydrangeas are heavy feeders and respond well to applications of a complete fertilizer. Blindness in hydrangeas is often caused by lack of phosphorus and potash.

Color change can be effected through the use of aluminum sulfate—one pound to five gallons of water applied one pint per plant a week. This makes the soil very acid (pH 5.5 or lower). Medium and light pink hydrangeas turn a clear blue under the treatment; deeper-colored varieties turn purple and lavender. Where aluminum is present in large quantities in the soil, the color of pink varieties is improved by the addition of hydrated lime at the rate of half a teaspoon once a week.

Kalanchoe—KALANCHOE BLOSSFELDIANA

Before the poinsettia became widely known, this plant was very popular for Christmas. It literally becomes covered with small bright red flowers. Plants are easily propagated from seeds and make better specimens than those grown from stem or leaf cuttings. Grow them in a cool or warm greenhouse.

Practically any kind of soil will do, but provide good drainage. Applications of liquid fertilizer in spring and summer are beneficial. Full sunshine is needed to produce stocky, compact growth and well-formed flowers. Three or four plants of dwarf Tom Thumb in a 6-inch bulb pan make a good show, but for the finest flowers—bigger than the old-fashioned kind—grow Brilliant Star.

Poinsettia—EUPHORBIA PULCHERRIMA

Buy yourself plants from seedsmen in fall, or propagate your own from cuttings in June, July, and August. Few plants root so easily. After flowering, old plants that are to be used for cutting-stock can be placed under the bench and given only enough water to keep stems from shriveling. In April they should be repotted in new soil and cut back. Syringing will encourage new growth. Cuttings root easily in a shaded propagating bench.

Grow in a mixture of three parts fibrous loam and one part sand. Free drainage is a must. Pinch up to the end of August to encourage side branching. Superphosphate or horn meal can be added to the potting soil—a 4-inch pot to a bushel—and applications of liquid fertilizer will give the plants a good boost. They should begin to show color by December 1st for bloom by Christmas.

Never try to grow poinsettias in a cool greenhouse. Most varieties require a temperature of at least 60°. Sudden drops in temperature, drafts, and overwatering will cause the foliage to turn yellow and drop. And a poinsettia without foliage is a funny looking sight! I know, having had many go that way.

Primrose—PRIMULA OBCONICA *and* P. MALACOIDES

It only takes a few plants of malacoides primroses in their new luminous shades to make the greenhouse sparkle with color. The obconicas are showy, too, but not so popular because of the skin irritation they frequently cause.

Sow seed of P. malacoides from May to October for

spring bloom. The earlier the sowing, the larger the plant. Sow P. obconica in May for flowering by Christmas and later. Transplant seedlings to 3-inch pots as soon as they can be handled easily. Use half soil and sand, for the fine roots need good drainage. Mix a complete fertilizer into the soil when making the final shift. Primroses are cool plants and will not prosper at night temperatures above 50°.

Roses

I always like to have a few pots of the smaller varieties of roses in the greenhouse. You don't get an abundance of flowers to cut, but there are plenty of buds for corsages all through winter. You can grow them in a cool or warm greenhouse but, since they prefer 60°, there won't be as many blooms at low temperatures.

Buy plants in fall and set them firmly in a 10- or 12-inch pot or tub, using loose fibrous soil with one-fourth part peat moss or rotted manure added. Place the plants in a coldframe under a 12-inch mulch, until roots form. The plants can be placed on their sides. Ramblers or climbers will have to be trained on a wire trellis.

In December, bring the plants into the greenhouse and set them under the benches. Wrapping the canes in burlap is a job, but beneficial.

When leaf buds are well formed, bring up into the light. Mulch the surface of the soil with rotted manure or peat moss. Feed periodically with liquid fertilizer and keep the foliage clean of insects and diseases with regular spraying. I have had particularly good success with Garnet, Siren, Pinocchio, Summer Snow, Red Sweetheart, Spartan and Vogue. Also recommended are Salmon Beauty, Margo Koster, Baby Rambler, and Gloire du

Midi. Hybrid teas can also be grown, but the few blooms hardly pay for the space.

During spring, cut plants well back and plunge to the rim in the garden. Keep them well formed with periodic pruning and free of mildew and insects by regular spraying. Top-dress, and bring them inside in fall; they will flower better the second year.

Schizanthus

This flower not only makes a good pot plant but can be grown for cut flowers. The dainty, small blooms, resembling orchids, are responsible for the common name, *Poor Man's Orchid.*

Sow in August or September for large potted specimens. Transplant into 3-inch pots and on up to 6- and 8-inch sizes, as required, pinching periodically to make the plants full and bushy. Either the tall or dwarf varieties make good pot plants.

For long-stemmed cut flowers, grow in benches, setting plants 8 inches apart. Short-stemmed blooms can be had from plants set 3 inches apart in deep seed flats. Grow at 50°. March and April is the flowering season.

Streptosolen—STREPTOSOLEN JAMESONII

This is a splendid small pot plant for the home greenhouse. It flowers freely during January with clusters of small deep orange blooms. The plants are self-perpetuating from cuttings during spring. Grow in a light sandy soil. Cut back after flowering to make good stocky growth for cuttings during the following season.

Wallflower—CHEIRANTHUS KEWENSIS

This attractive plant, 2½ feet high, has flowers which are light yellow on opening and mauve when more mature. Sow seeds in April, and set plants out in the garden during June. They should be potted in October and grown at a temperature of 45 to 50°.

Staking Potted Plants. By holding the end of the string in one hand and the ball in the other, the string can quickly be twisted around the stakes and tied to the stake at the starting point.

9

Orchids

YOU WILL FIND it fascinating to raise a few orchids in your greenhouse, no matter what other plants you grow. The chances are, once you have some in bloom, their glowing, rich colors and ethereal forms will win your heart so completely, that you will grow them exclusively. That has happened to many greenhouse owners.

With a collection of fifty or more well-selected plants, it is possible to have some in flower every day of the year. The blooms of some, such as Cymbidiums, last as long as three months.

Orchids are not the delicate plants we have often been led to believe they are. In fact, those usually grown under glass will stand more abuse than many of the annuals in your greenhouse. As with the other plants you grow, requirements of different genera vary in temperature, humidity, light, and moisture; and hybrids are affected according to their lineage, yet their needs are not too exacting. A number of plants with different habits may be grown together in the same greenhouse, for they will become adjusted to intermediate conditions.

The list of genera grown under glass is not long, but hybridization has produced an endless number of varieties that are far superior to their parents in color, form, and inflorescence. Most popular with amateurs as well as florists are the hybrid Cattleyas, Cymbidiums, Cypripediums, and Phalaenopsis. A knowledge sufficient to grow many orchids is not difficult to acquire. You will find orchid-lovers ever ready to discuss their favorite plants and give helpful advice. Caution should be taken in selecting your orchids, however, for some are much more desirable than others in beauty of color, quality of bloom, ease of handling, and period of flowering. It is advisable, therefore, to buy plants only from reliable sources.

The most popular orchids are the Cattleyas—the ones we see at parties, at the theatre, and in church. They are air plants or epiphytes that attach their fleshy roots to the bark of trees and in the moss and humus on the surface of rocks. They have leathery leaves and pseudobulbs which act as storage bins for food and moisture. Growth is made during the rainy season, and sufficient food is stored up to carry over through the dry season.

Orchids that have all their roots below the surface of the growing medium are classed as terrestrial. Calanthes and some of the Cypripediums or ladyslipper orchids are in this class. Semiterrestrials, such as Cymbidiums and other Cypripediums, get their nourishment from air roots and soil roots.

Conditions that are natural in the tropics are easily simulated in the greenhouse. Fresh air is supplied from roof ventilators. Side ventilation is seldom used because it decreases humidity. Ventilation is controlled all year round so that no cold air or hot drying breezes affect the plants. Humidity is kept dense by watering the walks and areas underneath the plant benches. Control can be manual or automatic. Some growers also use special humidifiers together with circulating fans that keep the air from becoming stratified.

In most localities the foliage is syringed during summer, and the osmunda is kept moist, except during the resting period that comes after flowering. Then water is withheld, but a humidity as high as possible is maintained, and the plants are syringed twice a day. The osmunda must never become entirely dry, and a shading is desirable most of the time.

Shade should be dense during spring, summer, and early fall, but less in late fall and winter. Roller slat shades are best for providing this. Of course, in areas such as along our West Coast, where there is a natural dense humidity and where prolonged periods of cloudy weather prevail, less water and less shading are needed, except during the hot summer. Water is not applied to foliage.

Fortunately, insects are not a serious problem with orchids, but they must always be kept under control. Thrips, scale, and weevil—the most common—are easily controlled with a malathion and DDT spray. Pests such as snails and slugs are easily controlled with a 15 per cent methaldehyde dust, or methaldehyde bait such as Buggeta pellets.

Orchid Benches

Special orchid benches provide the best conditions of humidity, drainage, light, and ventilation between plants. Half-inch-square mesh, galvanized-wire cloth is placed on top, or staging is built, as illustrated, with ½- by 1-inch redwood slats, placed ½ inch apart. A thick layer of gravel, coke, or osmunda is spread under the plant benches to hold moisture and increase humidity.

Propagation. Your orchid collection increases as you propagate new plants by division. This is done when the plants require repotting, normally at two to three year intervals.

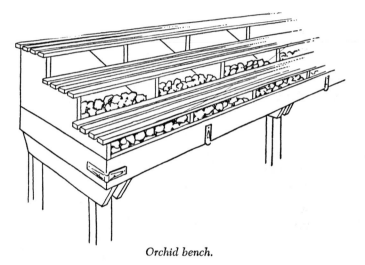

Orchid bench.

Cattleyas, and similar genera, generally make one new growth each year. In dividing the plant, the last four years' growth—four pseudobulbs—is potted up as the new plant. The old pseudobulbs—known as back bulbs—sometimes defoliated, are potted up and held in a warm humid atmosphere until strong new growth results.

Calanthes, and similar deciduous orchids, are propagated by rooting the back bulbs in sphagnum moss and sand, after their flowering period. The bases of the bulbs are placed about an inch deep in the sand, usually on an angle, with the eyes above the surface. When the roots are fully developed to an inch or more in length, the new plants can be potted and will flower the following winter.

Vandas, and other monopodials—those that make growth in an upright stem from year to year—develop air roots and shoots, at the axils of the leaves, and are propagated by air-layering. In the spring a cut is made partially through the stem at an axis, and sphagnum moss is wrapped around the cut and bound with waxed or linen thread. The moss is syringed frequently to keep it moist at all times, and when roots appear through the moss, the upper part is cut off and potted.

Potting. Amateurs often take their orchids to professionals for repotting, since special materials and handling are needed. Specialists themselves differ as to what is the best for individual genera. Osmunda fiber, which is the root of the cinnamon fern, is generally used in potting Cattleyas, Dendrobiums, and similar epiphyte orchids. It provides the free drainage needed by these plants that thrive mostly on air and water. The dark brown osmunda is preferred. It is first soaked in water, drained freely, and chopped or cut. The fine particles are removed and used for growing seedling plants.

Select a standard, orchid, or azalea pot. This should be large enough to allow for future root growth over a reasonably long period—usually two years—yet not so large as to permit the osmunda to remain soggy. Place plenty of small crock and charcoal in the bottom. Pack the osmunda fiber around the old root ball with a potting stick, working from the outside to the center. Pack firmly and evenly, being careful not to leave air pockets.

A well-potted plant will not drop out of the pot when

held upside down. Use shears to trim off the excess osmunda fiber. Curved shears are best. Stake and tie the plant with green florists' cord to keep the growth neat and straight. If possible, repot when the plant is dormant, but in plenty of time to have growth well established in the new osmunda fiber before winter. Shade the newly potted plants, and do not water the roots for a week or two, but syringe lightly once or twice, except in overcast or very cold weather.

Cymbidiums are usually potted in a mixture of two parts each of loam and osmunda fiber screenings, and one part each of sharp coarse sand and rotted cow manure. Of late, many growers are using less soil and mixing in redwood-bark shreds and leaf mold. Excellent response to feeding and tremendous blooms are reported. Repotting is done in spring. Ten- and 12-inch pots may be needed for mature plants. Commercial growers usually grow plants in ground beds.

Calanthes are grown in a mixture of one part each of coarse loam from composted sod or soil and manure, shredded osmunda, and well-rotted cow manure. Peat moss is sometimes used instead of osmunda.

Use a mixture of two parts fine shredded osmunda and one part each of loam from composted sod or soil and manure, and coarse sharp sand for Cypripediums.

In potting an orchid, just as with any pot plant, dividends in healthy, dark green foliage and beautiful, well-formed flowers are the reward for doing a good job. Poor potting results in dull, shrunken growth and small, misshapen blooms that are off color.

Orchids are far from expensive, unless you want to go in for the rare and unusual varieties. There are many splendid values in beautiful, small, blooming-size plants that can be had for an investment of possibly $200 to $300. Rod McLellan of South San Francisco, Calif., one of the largest orchid growers in the country, suggests the following varieties.

VARIETIES FOR THE BEGINNER

Cheaper

January	Cypripedium callosum—maroon, green and white (species)
February	Cattleya (hybrids)
March	Oncidium ampliatum—yellow with brown markings (species)
April	Cattleya Mossiae—medium lavender (species)
May	Brassolaeliocattleya Gordon Highlander—large labellum, lavender (hybrids)
June	Cattleya Alice Belding—white with colored lip (hybrids)
July	Cattleya Gaskelliana, lavender (species)
August	Phalaenopsis Skyline—white (hybrids)
September	Cycnoches chlorochilon—chartreuse (species)
October	Oncidium grande—yellow with brown markings (species)
November	Laeliocattleya Vandeletta—lavender with darker labellum (hybrid)
December	Cattleya White Fog—white (hybrid)

More Expensive

January	Cypripedium Maudia—green and white (hybrid)
February	Epidendrum Obrienianum—various colors (hybrids)
March	Vanda Rothschildiana—blue (hybrid)
April	Cattleya Mossiae—lavender (species)
May	Cattleya Life's Blood—lavender (hybrid)
June	Cattleya Hesperus—lavender (hybrid)
July	Oncidium Lanceanum—yellow and brown (species)
August	Cattleya Harrisoniana—mauve (species)
September	Brassocattleya Mt. Diablo—lavender (hybrid)
October	Oncidium grande—yellow and brown (species)
November	Brassavola Nodosa—white (species)
December	Cattleya Gail Ann—white (hybrid)

In making the above recommendations, Mr. McLellan does not recommend Odontoglossums or Miltonias for the mixed home greenhouse since they just don't do too well. This is also true of Calanthe which will not grow to perfection unless you have a warm compartment of 65 to

GENERA	TYPE	NIGHT TEMPERA-TURE	BLOOM
Brassavola	Epiphyte	55°-65°	Various
Calanthe	Terrestrial	65°-70°	White, rose, pink. Blooms in long racemes.
Cattleya	Epiphyte	55°-65°	Lavender, purple, rose-violet, yellowish-brown. Single or clustered blooms
Coelogyne	Epiphyte	55°-60°	White, greenish yellow with spotted lips
Cymbidium	Epiphyte and semiterrestrial	50°-55°	White, dull purple, crimson, brown and greenish yellow spikes
Cypripedium (Ladyslipper Orchid)	Mostly Terrestrial	60°-65°	Certain hybrids do very well at 60°-65° White, yellow, green, brown, purple
Dendrobium	Epiphyte	55°-60°	White & pink, White & lilac
Epidendrum	Epiphyte and semiterrestrial	55°-65°	Various
Laelia	Epiphyte	55°-60°	Rose lavender, blue, green, golden yellow, white, ivory
Lycaste	Epiphyte	50°-55°	Orange, yellow, white, rose. One or two blooms
Miltonia (Pansy Orchid)	Epiphyte	60°-65°	Single or in racemes. White, yellow, purple, rose, orange
Oncidium	Epiphyte	50°-60°	Yellow. Racemes of blooms
Phalaenopsis	Epiphyte	65°-70°	White, rose, purple. Racemes of flowers
Sophronitis	Epiphyte	55°-65°	Various
Vanda	Epiphyte	65°-70°	White, blue, green, lilac
Zygopetalum	Epiphyte and semiterrestrial	55°-65°	Various

70°. I have, however, seen a number come into flower in a 62° house, but they come in a month or so late.

When you buy orchids over and above the standard types, the difference in value is for exceptional merit and superior quality of bloom. This usually takes the form of good flower substance, excellence in shape, size, and harmony of color. The more nearly perfect the flower, the higher the price. Of course, in some instances, the mere fact that the plant is scarce makes it high priced. There are plenty of hybrid Cattleyas, Phalaenopsis, Cypripediums, and Cymbidiums that are outstanding in quality, and more are being added each year.

Note: Hybridization has upset temperature requirements, just as it has changed colors. Some deviation can be expected, therefore, in the plants found in the usual home greenhouse, unless a collection of species is grown. Usually, the blooms of the species are not of sufficient quality to attract the home gardener, except as botanicals or exotics of unusual interest.

10

Bulbs: Hardy and Tender

No OTHER GROUP of plants you can grow will give you so much beauty and pleasure for so little effort as the flowering bulbs. There is a vast, dependable assortment of bulbs to choose from that grow quickly and make a brilliant show throughout the winter.

All of those covered here are not true bulbs, but to avoid being technical, the term *bulb* is used for all. Yet, there are differences. A true bulb is made up of fleshy layers or scales and has a flower or leaf bud inside, such as the bulb of a hyacinth, tulip, or daffodil. A corm is a hard, underground stem or portion of root, like the so-called bulbs of the gladiolus, freesia and crocus. A rhizome is a thick, fleshy root, such as the root of achimenes and iris. Tubers are swollen fleshy roots, many of which contain eyes. Dahlias and ranunculus are grown from tubers.

Both the hardy and tender bulbs include many varieties which are easy to plant, to take care of, and to rely on for a succession of bloom. They require less attention than most plants and there is a wide selection to grow at cool to moderate temperatures of 45 to 60°. Of course, most of them can be brought into flower faster at higher temperatures (60°), or by applying hot water, but the flowers are sturdier and last much longer when the plants are grown slowly.

Insects and diseases are no problem if good clean bulb stock is bought from reliable dealers. It is not necessary to buy the jumbo-size bulbs, but it does pay to grow large-size bulbs raised especially for winter forcing.

Hardy Bulbs

Tulips, Hyacinths, and Narcissus

Pot up bulbs as soon as you receive them. Late September through November is the season. The longer the bulbs are left unplanted, the more they soften, and deteriorate. Fertility of soil used for them is less important than when other plants are grown, since the true bulb itself contains a reservoir of food and an embryo flower.

A loose, coarse soil is suitable. Soil from the garden or from the previous year's bench crop is excellent. The addition of peat moss may prove beneficial since a continuous supply of moisture is wanted, and the soil should never be permitted to dry out.

The bulbs are planted quite close together, about half an inch apart, in bulb pans, or 4-inch-deep flats. They are then watered well. Be sure to label them. A root-making period of eight to twelve weeks is required before they can be brought into the warmth of the greenhouse. A well-drained bulb pit or coldframe makes an ideal storage place, but a trench dug out in the garden is perfectly satisfactory. The pans or flats must not be set on top of one another, but shelves may be provided if the pit is deep enough. A plan of the pit showing where each variety is stored will be helpful in locating the varieties wanted when you are ready to take them into the greenhouse for forcing.

A covering of 8 to 10 inches of straw, or leaves and soil, placed on top and around the sides of the containers, is satisfactory to prevent freezing. If a layer of sand or cinders, an inch or two thick, is first spread over the top of pots and flats, it separates the soil in them from the covering and makes handling much easier.

Freezing is not harmful with these hardy bulbs, but growth is better and faster when they are not allowed to freeze tightly; 35 to 45° is the optimum storage temperature. Mice and rats are fond of tulip bulbs, so some means of protection against them is advisable. Make a wire basket, or buy a repellent dust especially sold for this purpose.

In late December the first lot of bulbs may be brought inside for forcing. Place them out of the way under a bench, until top growth starts, then bring them up into the sunlight. It takes four or five weeks at 50 to 55° before flowering starts.

Other lots of bulbs may be brought in as desired. Those forced later in the season will flower in about two weeks because of their stronger root growth and the greater intensity of the sunlight.

If you want to save the bulbs, continue to keep the foliage growing after the flowers are gone. Give them sunshine and water, and plant them out in the garden as soon as the soil can be worked. They will flower outdoors the following year if they were not grown in high temperatures the previous year. While it is possible to force the bulbs the following year, the quality of the bloom hardly makes it pay, especially when the bulbs will do better out in your garden.

Blooms by Christmas are possible with precooled bulbs planted in late October for immediate forcing. They are available only in large quantities but your florist may sell you some from his supply. If not, place bulbs in a box of dry moss in the refrigerator for eight weeks at a temperature of 45 to 50°. There is no trick to it.

Among tulips, Darwins are excellent for forcing. Though later to bloom than other kinds, they are vigorous growers with lasting flowers in a good selection of colors. The early-flowering tulips are smaller and their flowers do not keep as well. Other types are Dutch and English Breeders, Rembrandts, Art Shades, Parrot and Cottage tulips that flower early in May, and double-flowered varieties. Since there are so many varieties, and since these are being improved upon from year to year, a list of those to grow is not of much value. Good old stand-bys which I grow include William Pitt, William Copeland, Clara Butt, and Bartigon among the Darwins, Inglescombe Yellow—a well-known Cottage forcer, Brilliant Star, Ibis, Keizerskroon, Van der Neer, and Yellow Prince for early varieties.

Among the narcissi and daffodils the larger trumpet varieties are most frequently forced. Good popular varieties like King Alfred, Emperor, Ben Hur, and Spring Glory never fail to make a show either in pots or as a cut flower. Spring Glory is used mostly for cutting, since it grows quite tall.

The medium-trumpet group gives us such beauties as

(*Above*) Martha, Laurens Koster, and Dante daffodils with William Copeland tulips, make handsome greenhouse plants for spring. (*Below*) Oxalis can be counted on to flower from bulbs throughout the year. (Author Photos)

(Above) When you grow orchids, you have one or another plant in bloom every day of the year. (Lord & Burnham Photo) *(Below)* Camellias are handsome shrubs for the cool greenhouse. (Roche Photo)

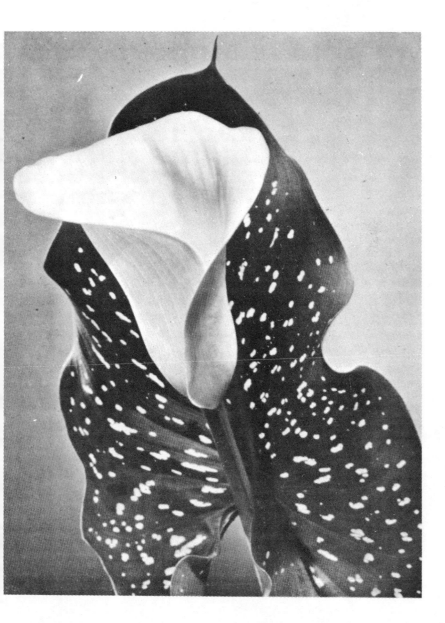

The yellow or golden calla lily, grown from a tender bulb, offers dramatic contrast of flower and leaf for the warm greenhouse. (Roche Photo)

When planting hardy bulbs, first partially fill clay pans or pots with soil, and set bulbs on top.

(Below) Add soil to fill the pot to tips of the bulbs and firm the soil between them.

(Below left) Place the pots in a coldframe or pit and protect with a layer of sand and of straw mulch.

(Below right) In eight to ten weeks, you can expect roots to have formed; shoots will appear. (R o c h e Photos)

Sir Watkin, with its extra-large petals; Martha, with its deep golden trumpet; and Diana Kastner, with a fluted, red cup. Von Sion is the well-known double, but the flower always seems too heavy for the stem. Golden Sceptre is a popular jonquil with sweet-scented flowers.

The poeticus varieties have a very small, red, fringed cup and white petals. Actaea and Horace are good. The poetaz or Poet's Narcissus is a cross between poeticus and Tazetta, of which Paperwhite is a variety. Laurens Koster and Orange Cup have beautiful buttercup-like flowers on strong stems.

Tender Bulbs

Tender and half-hardy bulbs such as amaryllis, nerine, freesias, ranunculus, anemone, and most of the lilies must not be permitted to freeze. Grow them in the greenhouse right from the start if you like, placing the pots under the plant benches until shoots appear. For me they do best when set in a coldframe under a deep mulch where they stay until it looks as if hard-freezing weather is on the way. Then they go under benches until top growth appears, when they are placed up in the light.

Paperwhite narcissus are grown in pots, flats, or benches right in the warmth, since they make growth so fast. Pebbles, moss, or soil can be used for the planting medium since it serves only to support the bulbs. They can be set halfway into the surface or just below.

See that they have plenty of moisture all the time. The flowers are ever so much fuller and prettier when grown in the greenhouse than in the house. I like to have several hundred Paperwhites. You will also find the following in catalogs: golden-orange Soleil D'or, the white and yellow Chinese Sacred Lily, and the dainty Roman hyacinths. The bulbs are inexpensive and are among the few you can easily bring into bloom for Christmas.

Achimenes

Achimenes have especially beautiful clusters of horn-of-plenty-shaped flowers in shades of crimson, rose, orange, blue, purple, and white, with eyes of contrasting colors. The rhizomes are started in March and April in shallow flats containing moderately moist sand and peat moss. Grow at 65 to 70°.

Set about ten or twelve in a 6-inch pan. Good drainage is essential so grow them in peat moss and sand or in a mixture of loose fibrous loam with one-fifth each of sand and peat moss. Feed with liquid manure or ammonium sulfate every other week until flowering.

Succession of bloom from early summer to fall is possible by starting plants at different intervals. The rhizomes may be grown the following year, if water is reduced after flowering to dry them off gradually. Then remove from pots, clean, and store in a bag or box of sand in a cool place, about 45 to 50°. Achimenes are also started from seed in January and February.

Amaryllis

The amaryllis is one of the most spectacular blooms you can grow in your greenhouse—an enormous lily-like flower in white, or various shades of pink to brilliant red, as well as white striped with red. The bulbs are planted from late October to December in fibrous sod loam. Ohio State University recommends a 4-inch pot of 2-10-10 fertilizer added to a wheelbarrow of soil, for amaryllis needs phosphorous and potash.

The bulb is planted about one-third to one-half its depth below the soil. Holland-grown bulbs are expensive but well worth the price. The blooms are large, in beautiful colors, and you have them as early as Christmas. The ordinary kind would flower in late January or February.

The foliage continues to grow after flowering, and ample moisture is needed for its development. Toward fall when the leaves begin to go, the bulbs should be dried off gradually and finally stored so they can rest on their sides until December when new growth will appear.

Because of the benefit the plant may receive from the old roots, it is a much-debated point whether they should be potted in new soil or grown on in the old with top dressing added. My own experience has been that they do better when repotted in new soil.

Amazon Lily—EUCHARIS AMAZONICA *and* GRANDIFLORA

This favorite, also known as star of Bethlehem, is an excellent bulb bloom to grow in the warm greenhouse for more reasons than one. It gives you beautiful, fragrant, pure white flowers on graceful foliage in late winter, and if dried off after flowering, good bulbs will often produce another crop in spring.

Plant bulbs in early summer, placing several in a large pot for a good show. Use a loose, rotted-sod loam and manure, adding sand, if necessary, to make the soil porous. Keep the soil slightly moist until growth starts in summer. Then give plenty of water and shade from the heat of midday sun.

In fall, place the plants in sun in a cool part of the house (55°), and hold back on the water gradually, but never allow the soil to become bone dry. About midwinter, place the plants in a warmer (65°) part of the house, and give them a thorough soaking.

Anemone—ANEMONE CORONARIA

These brilliantly colored poppy-like flowers are a must in the cool greenhouse. The best blooms are grown from seed sown in late spring, but it is easier to raise them from corms. Seeds should be sown in clay bulb pans taking special precautions against damp-off as described in Chapter 19. When young plants are large enough, transplant about 4 inches apart in the bench or deep clay pans.

If you use corms, you will find they are pointed on one end. Press them into the soil with the point down. Start corms during September or October in rich, fibrous sod loam lightened with one-fifth sand and one-fifth peat moss or leaf mold. Fill the bulb pans up to ¾ inch from the rim, and press the tubers into the soil about 2 inches deep and an inch apart. The delicate growth is subject to damp-off, so spread ¼ inch of clean sand over the surface of the soil. Water moderately and store the pans under a bench or in a coldframe to make roots. As soon as growth starts, bring up in the light. Flowering starts in January or February.

After flowering, the corms can be cleaned, stored in a cool place and forced again, but new ones are so inexpensive that this is hardly worth while. Popular varieties are St. Brigid, De Caen, Blue Poppy, and Sulphide.

Blood Lily—HAEMANTHUS

This is one of the most fascinating flowers you can grow. It has a ball-shaped bloom containing 100 to 150 star-shaped flowers borne on a single stout stalk. There are a number of kinds with different growing habits. H. multiflorus is red and blooms in the spring before foliage appears; it is dormant in winter. The scarlet H. coccineus is fall-flowering, also before foliage appears, and is dormant in summer. H. Katharinae with red blooms in spring is practically evergreen and should not be dried off. Grow at 50 to 60°.

Blue African Lily—AGAPANTHUS AFRICANUS

Here's a good blue flower for late spring. It is available in many hybrid forms, and as most grow quite large, the smaller varieties, such as My Joy, are most suitable for a small space. Water well during spring and summer, but very little when it is resting during fall and midwinter. Grow at 45 to 55°.

Calla Lily—ZANTEDESCHIA AETHIOPICA

The callas are good to grow because they require so little attention. The flowers last a long time when plants are grown slowly, and the plant continues to provide attractive and useful foliage after the flowers are gone.

The rhizomes may be potted up any time from August through December. Smaller ones can go into 5- or 6-inch pots. The larger ones will need 7- or 8-inch sizes. They are not fussy as to soil, and your regular compost should prove excellent.

Callas will grow in any temperature from 50 to 70°, but the flowers will have more substance and last longer when grown at 50 to 55°. The rhizomes should be watered sparingly until growth starts. Then they can take more water and will be benefited by one or two feedings of ammonium sulfate solution or a complete liquid fertilizer. After flowering, dry off by withholding moisture until the following season.

Zantedeschia aethiopica is the well-known, stately, white variety that grows 2 to 3 feet tall. Z. Elliottiana is the yellow or golden lily which has spotted leaves. Z. macrocarpa, often listed as Z. Pentlandii, is deeper yellow with leaves of solid green. Z. Rehmannii is a baby calla, with pink to rose flowers. It grows 12 to 15 inches high. Z. melanoleuca is the black-throated calla. It is yellow with a splotch of purplish black inside.

Many hybrids, which make most interesting novelties to grow, are to be found in seed and bulb catalogs and for sale at flower shows. Try a few dwarf pinks, purples, and pale blues when you come across them.

Cape Cowslip—LACHENALIA

Another old favorite with bell-shaped blooms in tiers along a 9-inch scape is the cape cowslip. There are both erect and pendulous varieties in a wide range of colors. These are all excellent as pot plants or for hanging baskets. Bulbs planted in August or September are set in a coldframe to make growth until November or December. Then they are brought into the greenhouse and grown at 50°. Avoid drafts. After flowering when leaves have died back, store in the same pots and soil until the following August.

Clivia Miniata

Popular for large bright clusters of orange-yellow blooms on a stiff upright stem 2 feet tall. Good hybrids are available. Foliage thrives at a temperature of 60° while making growth in spring. A temperature of 45 to 50° is better in fall and winter when the plant rests and wants just enough water to prevent leaves from wilting. The heavy leaves are beautiful for flower arrangements.

Crinum

This is another large bulb-plant, so you won't want many. It throws up a long stem with six to twelve fragrant lily-like trumpets in late spring or summer. The bulbs are handled like amaryllis and may be completely dried off after flowering or grown on slowly through the year for their decorative foliage. Grow at 55 to 60°.

Crocus

Pot crocuses in September and set them in the cold-frame for at least six weeks. About eight to ten corms may be planted in a 5-inch pot. Grow them in a 45 to 55° house. Select corms raised especially for forcing. They come in many shades of blue, red, lilac, purple, and in white.

Dahlia

Dahlia fanciers appreciate the greenhouse as a means of propagating new and rare varieties. Propagation may be started in February by dividing the tubers and rooting cuttings. The tubers are placed in moist sand in a 55 to 60° greenhouse. When the shoots develop about four leaves, a cut is made through the node. The cuttings are then rooted in sand, or sand and peat, with a bottom heat of 65 to 70°. Electric soil-heating cable is excellent for this purpose. As soon as the cuttings are rooted they may be potted in a rich medium soil.

Freesia

You miss something really worth while if you don't grow a few pots of freesias. The foliage is scraggly and unattractive, but the blooms are fragrant and lovely. You can have them for cutting by Christmas, if you plant corms in August and grow them 55° to 60°.

Potting Freesias.

Fill the pans or flats with four parts light soil mixed with one of peat moss or leaf mold. The corms are pressed into the soil with the point up. Water well and place under the greenhouse bench or in a pit or coldframe with deep mulch protection. Do not water again until growth starts. Grow at any temperature from 48 to 60°. Flowers can be had from late December into March.

Supports are needed. Use bamboo stakes and string, or lay a half-inch-mesh wire on top of the pan and raise this on stakes as plants grow. The white freesias are the most popular. Elder's Giant White and Elder's Double White are better varieties than the old stand-by, Purity. Marie Louise Fischer and Miss Blanche Blue are light blue; Sunset, Golden Wonder, and Elder's Judy are yellow.

Gladiolus

The baby glads are best in the greenhouse, but don't start them too early. January or February is plenty of time.

Any medium-textured soil is suitable. Buy corms especially grown for forcing, setting them about 2 inches deep and 2 inches apart. Large-flowering varieties grown in benches should be set in rows about 6 inches apart. Grow at 50° using bottom heat to promote earliest flowering. Catalogs of greenhouse seed-and-bulb dealers offer good selections.

G. tristis concolor is one of the finest bulb plants. It has cream-colored blooms, resembling large freesias, on long stems. It has a most delicate fragrance at night and is called evening flower. Bulbs started in December can be flowered by February to late spring. After blooming, corms may be set out in the garden until the following fall. Grow cool—50°.

Glory Lily—GLORIOSA ROTHSCHILDIANA

Here are beautiful, rich-toned, golden-crimson blooms on long, climbing stems. The flowers are very popular for corsages. Petals curve back and accent permanent stamens. Several varieties are available.

Start in December or January for blooms by March. The tubers are long and take a deep pot. Grow at 60°. After flowering when foliage turns yellow, store tubers dry until fall.

Glory of the Sun—BRODIAEA UNIFLORA

An attractive blue cup-shaped flower, also known as star flower, is easy to grow in the 50° greenhouse. Plant the corms in August or September about 1½ inches apart in a pot or bulb pan, and handle like freesias.

Guernsey Lily—NERINE SARNIENSIS

Pink to scarlet blooms with recurved petals appear on a leafless stem 1 to 2 feet high. Most varieties bloom from September to November. Their beauty of form and exquisite color makes a combination that is highly sought. It is vital to good blooms that bulbs be given a long rest after drying off. Grow cool—50°.

Iris

Dutch, English, and Spanish bulbous iris are suited for winter flowering in the greenhouse. Wedgwood, Imperator, White Excelsior, and Yellow Queen are fine varieties. They are grown for cut flowers in flats or bulb pans.

Plant the bulbs during September about 2 inches apart and 3 inches deep. Water thoroughly and treat the same as tulips and narcissus. Start bringing them into the greenhouse in November. They grow best at a temperature of from 45 to 50°.

Lilies

Most of us don't think of greenhouse lilies in terms of brilliant color, but there is a terrific splash to be had with the new Jan de Graaff hybrids. Try 25 to 50 pots some year, along with 10 to 15 of the usual florist varieties. They all respond to the same treatment and it is exhilarating to have rich yellows, reds, and oranges in large, well-shaped blooms. They seem all the more colorful against the whites which I always grow for contrast.

Of the 40 different hybrids I have grown, I like the deep shades best. Those that did especially well were the following: the upright, fiery Indian-red flowers of Campfire; Fireflame with outward facing mahogany red blooms; Joan Evans, a golden yellow that flowers later; and Pagoda, a chrome-orange with lots of well shaped blooms. But whichever you choose, you'll have variation to your planting.

Some of the new primulinum are also worth a try, but for me they were a little finicky as to soil moisture and water, though some of the failures may have been due to the quality of the bulbs.

Of the florist's types, the Croft lily has always given me the greatest number of blooms and the most luxuriant foliage. Peerless blooms earlier but has fewer flowers. Lilium auratum, the fragrant gold-band lily, which is pure white with a yellow center, and L. rubrum, the speckled lily, are the most magnificent of all.

Lily bulbs are never really dormant and should be potted as soon as received. September and October are good months to start, although the auratums and regals are better put in during August, for these lilies take 16 to 18 weeks from planting to bloom for the best development. You could wait until October or November to put in Croft or Peerless lilies, but for blooms by late February and March, the newer hybrids should go in during late September or early October.

Of course, precooled bulbs like your florist uses flower much earlier, but they are only sold in large quantities. There is no trick to precooling bulbs if you can beg space in the refrigerator. Simply place them in dry peat moss or sand and store at 31 to 40° for five weeks before planting.

The same loose soil mixture suits all these lilies equally well. I use two parts loam composted with one part manure as described in Chapter 6, but if the soil has much clay, some sand should be added. Plant the bulbs one to a 6-inch pot, water well and set in a cold frame under 10 inches of loose mulch to make roots. Never let the bulbs freeze, especially the tender kinds. Bring them into the greenhouse before deep freezing occurs. Place the pots under a bench until leaf buds show, then move up into sunshine. If long stems are wanted, leave the plants under the bench somewhat longer.

Feedings every two weeks with ammonium sulfate or nitrate of soda mixed one tablespoon to a gallon of water should be given when growth is about 4 inches high, for if the soil is acid and not fertilized, there is danger of leaf burn. When the plants are tall, this fertilizer should be strengthened with a tablespoon of soluble 5-10-5 applied about one-half pint to each plant.

After the lilies have bloomed, I have found it best to knock the bulbs out of the pots and set them in the garden in spring, as soon as weather permits. Here many will flower again in July or August.

Regardless of treatment, it never pays for me to force the same bulbs a second time. While they may succeed for years outdoors, in the greenhouse they are infested with mosaic.

Lily-of-the-Valley—CONVALLARIA MAJALIS

By successive planting lily-of-the-valley can be had in flower from January through May. These are grown from specially precooled bulbs or pips that came from Europe, especially Germany. Grow them in a box 8 inches deep, in a deep bulb pan, or in a bench if large quantities are wanted. Sand, peat moss, or sphagnum moss may be used as the planting medium.

The pips are planted with the crowns extending about ½ inch above the surface. Keep them covered with heavy paper for about two weeks, then gradually let them have full light. Bottom heat is wanted—about 70 to 80°. A covered propagating bench is a good place to grow them. Water heavily during this preliminary period, tapering off when the flower-buds appear. The pips are useless once they have been forced.

Ornithogalum

The fragrant clusters of cup-shaped blooms are so worth while you'll enjoy raising them in quantity. Bulbs are started in early fall for midwinter bloom.

The most commonly grown, and one of the showiest, is O. arabicum, which has large white flowers. Many other varieties are available. Foliage appears after the blooms and must be kept growing until spring. Then dry off gradually, and store bulbs right in the same pots until the following season. Grow at 55 to 65°.

Oxalis

A delightful subject for pots, hanging baskets, or a border along the edge of the benches. It is available in pink, white, or yellow and is grown from tubers. Grow in a soil that is light, and feed occasionally with liquid manure or ammonium sulfate. Some varieties such as O. rubra are everblooming and plants may be set out in spring, and they will bloom until you lift and bring them into the greenhouse in fall. Propagation is by division.

Other good varieties are O. cernua, the Bermuda Buttercup, with yellow flowers; O. hirta, which is rose-pink; O. lasiandra which is carmine; and the white O. Regnalli.

Ranunculus—RANUNCULUS ASIATICUS

Ranunculus are handled similar to anemone. They do quite well from tubers started in September or October but may be put in as late as November. Plant the roots 2 inches deep and about 2 inches apart in a clay bulb pan or seed flat. Set in a coldframe to make roots until January. Excellent plants can also be had from seed.

The plants do well in a rich, sandy loam. Care should be taken when watering for they are very susceptible to damp-off. Grow at 50° for flowers in March. Varieties I have grown with success include: Claremont Hybrids and Tecolote Giants.

Scarborough Lily—VALLOTA SPECIOSA

Here are scarlet lily-like flowers that appear in spreading clusters in spring or summer. This plant requires very little attention if perfect drainage is provided. Soil should be kept moderately moist during the winter rest. Grow at 50 to 55°.

Tritonia—TRITONIA CROCOSMAEFLORA

Pot up in October and handle the same as freesias, placing a large number of corms in a pot or bulb pan. They will flower in April in a 45 to 55° greenhouse. Flowers grow on fine branches, ten or twelve beautiful cup-shaped blooms to the branch. Colors are orange, yellow, and red.

Tuberose—POLIANTHES TUBEROSA

Buy only the best for forcing and pot them up in early spring, placing three bulbs to a 5-inch pot. Use a coarse loam with sand added if necessary to make it porous. Grow in a 55 to 60° house. Water heavily after growth starts, and never permit the soil to dry out. Flowers are white and delightfully fragrant.

Tulbaghia

This plant is practically everblooming with clusters of star-shaped lavender blooms on 18-inch stems. T. fragrans has very fragrant blooms, as the name implies. T. violacea blooms even more freely but has a vile onion smell if you break the foliage. Culture is the simplest ever—just pot up and grow in semishade during summer and in full sun the rest of the year. Grow cool—45 to 50°.

Veltheimia Viridifolia

It has a compact clustered head of drooping yellow blossoms tinged with red that resembles the red hot poker. Wavy, sword-shaped leaves are shiny and attractive all year.

Bulbs started in November or December will bloom any time from early or late spring, but you can also bring them into flower in December by keeping foliage in good growth throughout summer. Grow in full sunshine after flowering, and keep on the dry side until leaves turn yellow and die back. Then dry off completely. Grow at 50°.

Flowering Shrubs and Perennials

Hardy Flowering Shrubs

THERE ARE A LARGE number of hardy shrubs that can be forced into bloom during winter in the greenhouse. Almost any that flower early in spring out of doors are suitable—azaleas; clematis; daphne, both Cneorum and Mezereum; the various deutzias, including gracilis and Lemoinei; syringa; flowering plums, cherries, and crabs; rhododendron; mountain laurel; forsythia; Japanese maples—Acer japonicum and A. palmatum; Philadelphus Lemoinei; dogwood; weigela and many others.

Prepare the shrubs a year in advance of forcing. Young plants are the best and they should be trimmed, dug, and planted in pots or tubs right after the flowering season in spring. All useless branches should be removed and an attractive, compact, symmetrical appearance achieved in the pruning.

During summer, the pots may be plunged to the rim in the garden to hold in moisture. But do not neglect to water, syringe, and spray for insects.

The flowering maple (Abutilon) has showy crimson, yellow, and white
flowers and grows readily from seed. (Roche Photo)

SOWING SEEDS I

Fill bulb pan with good compost; level off with stick; tamp firmly but not too hard.

(Below) Sow fine seed broadcast, as pictured; but sow large seed in rows. Cover with sphagnum moss or clean sand to help prevent damping off. (Author Photos)

SOWING SEEDS II

Water gently with a bulb or by subirrigation. Glass placed on top helps hold in moisture and keep temperature even. *(Center)* A good stand; it is cauliflower. *(Below)* Shade to slow up evaporation; transplant seedlings when large enough to handle. (Author Photos)

(Above) A sowing of coleus seed produces a crop of handsome, variegated-leaved plants. *(Below)* Cinerarias in white and pink-to-purple shades are fine to grow from seed; plants flower for a month or more. (Roche Photos)

In fall, the wood should be permitted to harden off naturally out of doors. Then the plants may be moved to a storage pit or cellar. A temperature just above freezing is best during storage—about 35°. It should never be warm enough to allow top growth to form. If a cellar or pit is not available, however, a well-drained trench will serve just as well. A heavy mulch of straw placed around the pots or tubs will provide ample protection and make handling easy. The plants do not require watering during this period, but must not dry out completely.

After the middle of January they can be brought into the greenhouse for forcing. They should be brought into the heat gradually by placing them at the cool end of the greenhouse first. A temperature of 45° is desirable.

Plants will force at temperatures of 50 to 60°. The plants brought in during midwinter will take two to three months to bloom. Those brought in during March will flower in about four weeks and are a better bet for good results. Syringing daily with warm water is helpful in making the leaf buds appear. Biweekly watering with liquid manure or ammonium sulfate should also be carried out.

In spring, the plants may be planted out. Many varieties are not suited to forcing the following year, but if transplanted occasionally to maintain a good root ball they may be placed in a pot or tub and forced again.

Tender Flowering Shrubs

Acacia

This is a beautiful flowering shrub or tree with gray-green foliage on graceful branches that become covered with tiny clusters of yellow flowers. Those most desirable for greenhouse culture come from Australia. A. armata or A. Drummondii are delightful as pot plants; A. pubescens grows in long sprays and is not so well suited for the small greenhouse since it soon requires considerable head room.

Propagation is from the cuttings of side shoots, but since it takes two years to produce a satisfactory plant, it is far better to buy a few small ones from your seed house. Propagation is easy, however, at any season. When the plants are potted, a temperature of 45° is desirable. In early spring they should be set outdoors, where even a touch of frost will do no harm. Ample moisture is needed during summer, which is the time most growth is made. In fall, the plants are repotted and grown on in the greenhouse.

Camellia—CAMELLIA JAPONICA

The camellia has recently become one of the most popular of flowering shrubs, and rightly so. It is easy to grow in the small greenhouse, and there is no flower more appropriate or lovely to wear on any occasion, or to arrange in shallow vases for the table, window sill or mantelpiece. The fact that it is a member of the tea family accounts for the dark green, glossy leaves which make such an attractive setting for the blooms. These vary from white and soft shades of pink to brilliant red. Not only are they rich-looking, but they have substance, and while not so fragrant as the hard-to-grow gardenia, they keep much better when cut, often as long as a week.

Buy good plants from a specialist. With six or more selected varieties having different flowering periods, you can have blooms to cut from October through April. Grow them at 42 to 45° for the choicest flowers, but 50°

is satisfactory. High temperatures, fluctuation in temperature, and drafts cause bud-drop.

A soil mixture of one-quarter peat moss and composted sod with sufficient coarse sand to make a light mixture is used for potting, but the soil must be acid—pH 4 to 5. Aluminum sulfate increases acidity, and can be added at the rate of eight ounces to a bushel of soil or one ounce to a gallon of water, to be applied when watering. The soil should be porous and well provided with good drainage, so it can be kept evenly moist throughout the tub. Placing the tub on legs is necessary so that water cannot settle in the bottom and make the soil become soggy and toxic. When growth starts, plenty of moisture is wanted. Maintain a humidity of 50 per cent, and syringe the foliage and buds regularly—about twice a day, right up until the flowering period.

After the plants have flowered, increase the temperature to 55°, if possible, and feed with ammonium sulfate —one level tablespoon to one gallon of water—or use a complete liquid fertilizer. The faster you get plants into growth, the earlier they flower the following season.

During spring and summer, plants will do best under semishade; a lath house or bamboo shades suspended over a frame give the right protection. Occasional trimming and syringing with water under pressure is the only additional care needed, except an occasional spray once or twice for scale, red spider, and mealy bug. DDT and strong insecticides must be used with caution since they cause burning.

When repotting is necessary, it should be done in early spring just after growth starts. Pack the soil firmly about the roots with a potting stick. If repotting is not necessary, top-dress with fresh soil. A mulch of peat moss, pine needles, or well-rotted manure is useful to maintain an even soil moisture.

Gardenia

The beginner will do well to shy clear of gardenias, for they are temperamental and difficult to grow. A plant will appear to be doing well right up to the production of good-looking flower buds, and just when you begin to count your blooms they drop off or become hard for no apparent reason. In spite of this warning, however, I have seen fine specimens raised by amateurs, and when well grown they really are lovely.

An acid soil consisting of one-quarter to one-half peat moss and silty loam is used for gardenias. A temperature of 65 to 70° must be maintained at all times. Gardenias cannot stand drafts or sudden changes in temperature. Feeding every other week with ammonium sulfate, one ounce to two gallons of water, is beneficial. Water should not be permitted on the foliage in winter, but a dense humidity is necessary.

Veitchii and Belmont are the varieties usually grown. They may be propagated from cuttings from December to March, but it is better to buy plants in 3- or 4-inch pots, grown by professionals, and grow them along up to flowering size. The plants must be shifted often and never be permitted to become pot-bound. In summer, gardenias make good growth out of doors. Side shoots and flower buds should be removed until late August, when the plants are again moved into the greenhouse. They can be grown for several years, but young plants produce best. Mealy bug is the most serious enemy.

Spirea—ASTILBE JAPONICA

Spirea is a hardy perennial that can be forced into bloom to give you desirable pot plants with spikes of white or light and deep pink flowers. Buy clumps in November, pot tightly and store them in the coldframe until the end of January, when leaf buds will have formed. At 55° they will flower in ten to twelve weeks. Applications of ammonium sulfate or manure water are beneficial. They like plenty of moisture, and must never be allowed to dry out. Pots can be set in saucers of water or, better yet, plants may be grown in pots equipped with glass wicks as described in Chapter 20. Green fly is a troublesome pest. The plants can be set out in the garden in spring, and divided and potted in November. Gloria Superba is deep pink; Queen Alexandra, light pink; Deutschland, white.

Perennials

Many of the perennials and biennials you grow in the summer garden make excellent material to grow under glass. There are dianthus, caesius and plumarius; hepaticas and trilliums; cypripediums in variety; columbine— Aquilegia canadensis; phlox, divaricata and subulata; primula, polyantha and veris; violas; campanula; shasta daisies; painted daisies; delphinium; gaillardia; and many others.

They are best when the plants are started from seed especially for the purpose. Seed should be sown early in February or March to produce large plants for forcing, though it is possible to force plants from the outdoor garden by digging them late in the year after a good frost. Pot the plants in good, medium light soil, and store them in the coldframe under a thick straw mulch. They can be brought into the greenhouse any time after mid-January. Grow them slowly in a temperature of 45 to 50°. Perennials grown this way usually produce larger and better flowers than those grown out of doors.

Flowering Climbers and Twiners

Don't be afraid to try some of the handsome climbing plants. Even the most vigorous are easily kept from growing rampant when roots are confined to pots or tubs, and branches are well pruned and trained. Many climbers that reach 10 to 20 feet and more, in the tropics, can be flowered in a 5- to 10-inch pot on a 4- to 5-foot trellis; more delicate twining plants can be restricted still further.

You will find a splendid selection for numerous purposes. Hang them from shelves and over the sides of benches, twine them up wire to the braces and rafters, or over low trellises. Nothing does more to soften harsh lines and give a pleasing touch to the greenhouse.

Some tying may be needed to train the vines. Use florist's green wire, string, raffia or Twist-ems. Fasten to the support first, then tie with a loose loop around the branch, but tie singly and never bunch stems together.

The majority of these plants do well in the same pot for several years, if you feed them periodically when they are making growth and top-dress with fresh soil each fall

143

or spring. When old plants become hard and leggy, discard them. Cuttings can easily be rooted from well-ripened wood taken three or more joints down from the terminal, but you will not want the same climbers all the time and will often discard old for new.

Hoya carnosa is an excellent plant for the beginner to start with and twine up into the rafters. It has fleshy green leaves and is so rugged a plant it reaches up to 15 or more feet when grown in a large pot or tub, but mine in a 5-inch pot never reaches more than 6 to 8 feet. The flower clusters that appear in late spring or summer are fragrant and waxy in white-tinted pink.

The leadwort plant (plumbago) is another easy one that does well in a 5- or 6-inch pot. I grow it on a shelf to lend grace to the severe line of the greenhouse eave. The clustered azure-blue flowers are especially desirable and follow one another on the tips of every branch from spring to late fall.

Jasmine, a fine climbing plant, also blooms for us from spring until late fall and is tops for delicate fragrance. It is a cool greenhouse plant. Flowers drop off at high temperatures, but it is worth trying even in a moderately warm house. Jasminum officinale is the climber with fragrant white flowers but there are several others. J. Sambac is a fragrant, double, white twiner.

The star jasmine (Trachelospermum jasminoides) is one of my favorites and has done beautifully in the same 4-inch pot for three years. It flowers intermittently from early spring to late fall, with clusters of small white fragrant stars at practically every joint. You have only to rest it in a semidormant state by withholding water for a week or two to bring it into bloom again. A 2-foot fan-trellis makes a good support, and if any of the wiry growth reaches out too far, you simply snip it off.

Several fine climbers tend to be too large for the small greenhouse and, if you grow them, you must not expect the profusion of bloom you see pictured in the catalogs. Some of the allamandas, bougainvilleas, and stephanotis, are examples.

Allamanda (A. cathartica Williamsii) with long yellow flowers is a beautiful plant for the north end of a medium-sized greenhouse, but it should have a ground-bed or large tub; A. neriifolia and A. violacea are more suitable.

Bougainvillea, Crimson Lake, with beautiful bracts of rosy red is suitable as a pot plant, but most of the others grow too large. Stephanotis with lovely, fragrant, white flowers in summer, could be grown, but blooms will not be plentiful.

The passion flowers are also vigorous, but can be kept under control. Try one or two on a fan-shaped trellis. They require little care and the spectacular flowers never fail to be conversation plants. As I write this (January 15, 1955), I have Passiflora grandiflora on a 3-foot trellis with sixteen buds about ready to open. I also have P. trifasciata, the one with the variegated foliage, and it promises to be lovely but is far more delicate.

Foliage Plants

No MATTER HOW determined you are to specialize in certain flowers, you need attractive foliage plants to lend grace and charm to the greenhouse. The catalogs of specialists illustrate a tremendous assortment, and fascinating introductions appear each year. You will find sizes, shapes, leaf patterns, and colors for practically any purpose or location. There are hanging plants for shelves and baskets, creepers to soften the edges of benches, twiners for trellises or totem poles, vigorous climbers that reach to the rafters, sprays and upright foliage to cut for bouquets, corsages, and flower arrangements.

Foliage plants are handsome the year round, require less attention than flowering plants, and succeed under conditions where other plants won't grow. They are especially appropriate for greenhouses that do not have a sunny exposure, for most of them will do well without direct light. You can even grow them *under* the benches, and in summer many will flourish in spite of the hottest weather, if given ample moisture, ventilation, and shade.

A glassed-in room with such planting often becomes the most comfortable and attractive spot in the home.

Foliage plants also do wonders to brighten up certain spots in the house, and they last a long time. Whenever they show the least sign of shriveling, you have only to return them to the greenhouse for a period of rejuvenation. Practically all are easily multiplied by cuttings, so you can always have them in quantity to give away to friends. A gift plant in a gay pot or glass container is sure to make a hit.

Soil should be high in organic matter, so a large proportion of the mixture should be of peat moss or coarse leaf mold, acid soils being best. Good drainage and high humidity are essential. The pothos and peperomias do better, however, if foliage is not syringed, and soil is kept on the dry side.

Ivies are the most widely grown foliage plants and smaller-leaf varieties, the most attractive. You'll like them for baskets, pots, and as edgings both inside the greenhouse and outdoors. They are easily multiplied by cuttings either in propagating bed or coldframe and grow at temperatures from 45 to 50°.

There are a great many new types, with more coming out each year. Some of the choicest include Hahn's Pittsburgh Ivy, one of the best self-branching types; Merion Beauty, a compact variety with smaller leaves; Jubilee, variegated green-and-white small-leaved dwarf; Abundance, a new, compact, ruffled-leaf type; Pedata, small bird's-foot-shaped leaf with white veins; Pixie, dwarf and compact with ruffled leaf; Minima, bushy and very small-leaved.

Favorites among other vines are Philodendron cordatum and pothos, the devil's ivy, and there are many others. Here is a list of foliage plants from Prof. Alex Laurie, one of the largest dealers:

SMALL (vines and upright plants)

Cissus antarctica (kangaroo vine)
rhombilfolia
Dracaena Godseffiana
sanderiana
Maranta Kerchoveana
Nephthytis liberica
Green Gold
Tri-Leaf Wonder

Peperomia obtusifolia—green and variegated
Sandersii
Philodendron pittieri
sanguinolentus varifolium
Pothos goldiana (sport of Wilcoxi)
Silver Streak (sport of Silver Marble)
Syngonium Hoffmani
Wendlandii

LARGE (somewhat touchy in the house)

These plants are of a tropical nature. Most of them grow in the shade at warm temperatures. Direct sunlight in summer will damage them.

Philodendron Andreanum
cannifolium
dubium
erubescens

hastatum
panduraeforme
pertusum
trifoliatum

LARGE (tough)

These plants will stand temperature variations from 50 to 75° and can be kept on the dry side without appreciable damage but they do require shade.

Aspidistra lurida
Dracaena Warneckii
Ficus elastica
pandurata
Howea Belmoreana
Monstera deliciosa

Pandanus Veitchii
Philodendron bipinnatifidum
fosterianum
Wendlandi
Sansevieria Laurentii
zeylanica

The best of the lot is Philodendron Wendlandii. It is only good from seed but does well anywhere and will take abuse. Others in this group are Philodendron bipinnatifidum and fosterianum.

Hanging Plants for Shelves and Baskets

There are many attractive plants for shelves and baskets. I am fascinated by such trailers as rosary vine or string of hearts (Ceropegia Woodii); strawberry begonia (Saxifraga sarmentosa); Kenilworth ivy (Cymbalaria muralis); periwinkle (Vinca major); Sprenger asparagus fern (Asparagus Sprengeri); Selaginella uncinata; Ruellia Makoyana; necklace vine (Muehlenbeckia complexa); and wandering Jew (Tradescantia zebrina) that comes in so many forms.

Episcias make good hanging plants in the warm, shady greenhouse for shelves, baskets, or edging benches. You will frequently find them grown under the benches in orchid houses.

Among smaller upright plants you will enjoy aluminum or watermelon pilea (P. cadierei), but beware of the artillery plant (P. microphylla) for it becomes a terrible weed. Also in this group are Cryptanthus zonatus var. zebrinus; the umbrella plant (Cyperus alternifolius); seersucker plant (dichorisandra); blood leaf (iresine); prayer plant (maranta); and there is no end of fancy-leaved geraniums and begonias in the catalogs.

Crotons also offer the brightest of selections and there are thousands of patterns to choose from. You will be glad to have a few, if your greenhouse is warm enough, 65 to 70°. The leaves, often up to 18 inches, are colorful the year through and are just what is needed for many flower arrangements.

Fancy-leaved caladiums have leaves as bright as flowers and they last in the greenhouse for many months. Caladiums are mostly for summer but they can be enjoyed by March, if well-cured rhizomes are started in early February. When there are no flowers in bloom, they are indeed a welcome sight. They need a high temperature of 65°. Water them moderately until growth starts and treat like calla lilies. Alocasia, a caladium relative, is also becoming a favorite. Colors run to coppery tones with silver veins in the leaves. Grow in shade at all times.

Coleus gives you some handsome color designs, especially from a packet of Rainbow Mixed seed. They need a warm temperature to germinate—75°. There are large- and small-leafed strains, and the best are easily propagated from cuttings.

The foliage acalypha with colorful leaves can be grown in the same size pot year in and out. Only an occasional top-dressing is needed. Some have coppery green leaves, variegated with splashes of red; others are brown with a distinct red border. Give 55 to 65°.

Ferns do much for the greenhouse and you'll like them for background. Choose the more rugged types, like the Boston, maidenhair, bird's nest, and holly, unless you maintain a warm temperature. The majority of ferns like 60 to 65° with dense humidity, and while they may not suffer at 50°, they won't make growth. None are too fussy about soil, just use plenty of leaf mold or peat moss and mix in sand to assure free drainage. There are numerous small table ferns (pteris) that are pleasing for natural plantings in rough stone walls, rockeries, or terrariums. They are useful also to conceal the base of tall, bare-stemmed potted plants. One of the stag-horn ferns (platycerium) with antler-like leaves is also interesting in small pots.

Anthuriums need shade and a high humidity. They have handsome, large leaves with deep, thick veins. Others flower freely with bright red, orange-red, and salmon-colored blooms which last a long time. Unfortunately, many are inclined to grow too large for the small greenhouse, making it necessary to propagate new plants from root cuttings every few years. This is a plant that wants 60° and shade from early spring to fall.

The dieffenbachias are delightful with beautifully marked leaf patterns. The new varieties tend to chartreuse shades, but wide assortments are offered. When plants grow too tall with unsightly bare stems, just cut them off, replant the tops, and they will root again. The better ones are listed here:

D. amoena   D. picta
D. Bausei   D. Roehrsi
D. memoria corsi

14

Cacti and Succulents

A QUICK GLANCE through good cactus catalogs shows an endless quantity of fascinating plants to grow. You could easily fill a large greenhouse with them, yet hardly scratch the surface. The unique form and unpredictable manner these plants have throughout new growth, and their brilliant flower colors, never fail to stir the imagination. Try at least a dozen or more smaller types for those close-to-the-glass spots on your shelves and benches where they will fit in appropriately.

Some varieties are much better suited to greenhouses than others, so select those you can count on to grow well and flower most frequently. Take the popular prickly pear or opuntia, for example, which include the cinnamon cactus (O. rufida), old rabbit ears (O. microdasys), and O. santa-rita—all are interesting for form but seldom bloom under glass. This is also true of most of the lobivias. Only those in the list below flower well under glass, and among the epiphyllums only German Empress

Cacti and succulents make interesting cool greenhouse plants. This is one of the best stone mimickers. (Lithops summitatum)

A bench holds a collection of Echeverias. (*Below*) Tiger Jaws (Faucaria tuberculosa) blooms amid starfish leaves. (E. J. Alexander Photos)

In the cool green-house, Azalea indica flowers in white, pink, or rose shades.

A primrose makes an excellent pot plant for cool grow-ing in spring (Roche Photos)

Poinsettias are Christmas favorites for
the warm greenhouse. (Roche Photo)

The sturdy alamanda is a vigorous yellow-flowering vine for the large, warm greenhouse.

For the smaller, cool greenhouse, the delicate, yellow jasmine is a charming vine. (Roche Photos)

or Deutsche Kaiserin, plus a few other hybrids are really good.

Try not to let the jaw-breaking names scare you. There are good catalogs filled with detailed descriptions and illustrations so you will know what you are buying beforehand. Don't overlook the ten-cent stores as a source of supply, either.

I asked Edward J. Alexander of The New York Botanical Garden and Scott E. Haselton of the Cactus and Succulent Society of America (the most prominent authorities I know) for a list of the most appropriate varieties. The following suggestions and comments are theirs.

Astrophytum
   A. Asterias
   A. capricorne
   A. myriostigma
   A. ornatum
Chamaecereus
Conophytum
Coryphantha
Cotyledon
Crassula
Dudleya
Echeveria
Echinocactus
Echinocereus
Echinopsis
Epiphyllum
Euphorbia
Faucaria
Gasteria
Graptopetalum
Gymnocalycium

G. Baldianum
G. Bruchii
G. Damsii
G. Friedrichiae
G. Mihanovichii
G. Monvillei
G. multiflorum
G. Venturianum
Haworthia
Huernias
Hylocereus
Kalanchoe
Lithops
Lobivia
   L. aurea
   L. Backebergii
   L. famatimensis
   L. Hertrichiana
Mammillaria
   M. Bombycina
   M. bocasana

M. candida
M. elegans
M. elongata
M. Hahniana
M. kewensis
M. plumosa
M. rhodantha
M. zeilmanniana
Mesembryanthemum
Notocactus
   N. apricus
   N. caespitosus
   N. Graessneri
   N. Haselbergii
   N. Leninghausii
   N. mammulosus
   N. Ottonis
   N. rutilans

N. Scopa
N. tabularis
Parodia
   P. aureispina
   P. mutabilis
   P. sanguiniflora
Pleiospilos
Rebutia
   R. deminuta
   R. Kupperiana
   R. minuscula
   R. pseudominuscula
   R. senilis
   R. violaciflora
Sedum
Selenicereus
Stapelia
Trichocereus

Under glass those that can be counted upon to flower easily are the gymnocalycium in a wide range from white to brilliant red, especially G. Damsii, G. Friedrichiae, and G. Mihanovichii; the noctocactus, of which N. apricus, N. Ottonis, N. mammulosus, and N. Leninghausii are particularly attractive; along with any of the rebutias. All are quite small so many can be grown on shelves and benches close to the glass.

Select yuccas and hylocereus with care, for most of these soon grow too large for the home greenhouse. This also goes for most of the Aloes, but there are some good small ones.

Among the astrophytums, A. ornatum, A. capricorne, and A. Asterias are good; among the rebutias, R. minuscula, R. pseudominuscula and all the other varieties are good, as are the echinocactus, echinocereus, coryphantha, faucaria, and gasteria. The parodia must not be passed over, either, for the large 2- to 3-inch flowers of many are way out of proportion to the size of the plant.

There are many succulents which bloom readily in the greenhouse. The echeveria and kalanchoe all flower well in winter. Some of the echeveria produce blossoms from fall to late spring and, of course, the kalanchoe (see Chapter 8) can be selected for flowers from December through February. The sedums start to flower in early spring and continue until late fall. Colors range from white through all shades of yellow to red in a few species. There is even one species—Sedum caeruleum—with a pale blue flower. Other succulents that will flower in the greenhouse are the stoneface (Lithops), crassula, and gasteria.

How To Grow Them

Succulents are happy in a drier atmosphere than most plants. They want top heat, rather than bottom heat and good ventilation. The majority do well with full sun most of the year and half shade in summer. A temperature of 50 to 55° is about right if you place the tropical species at the warm end of the greenhouse and the temperate ones at the cool end.

Most of my friends who specialize in these plants, find this one soil mixture satisfactory for all plants: One-third fibrous loam, one part leafmold, one part coarse, sharp sand, and a liberal amount of ground charcoal. Some mix fine gravel with the sand. Ground limestone is also needed if the soil is acid.

Propagation is much easier than you might think. Seed of most varieties germinates in ten to twenty days. Use the same soil mixture described above, but screen out coarse particles. Dust the surface with fine charcoal to avoid damp-off. This is also beneficial to newly transplanted seedlings which are set about an inch apart in clean flats. Do not water for three days after transplanting; then just water moderately so the roots settle naturally into the soil. Be sure to shade, if the weather is bright and hot. When set in straight rows, the young upright plants make a fascinating sight—like soldiers on parade. Many varieties also root readily from cuttings. Start with dry sand or soil. With cacti do not water for two or three weeks; with other succulents three or four days. This gives the cut a chance to heal and avoids stem rot.

The sedum, mesembryanthemum, kalanchoe, and many crassula are most easily propagated from leaves or root divisions, while agave, echeveria, gasteria are multiplied by offsets. Be a little gentle when making separations and pot singly.

From fall to spring, water can be withheld almost entirely from winter-dormant varieties. Any tendency for plants to shrivel soon disappears with a little water. Most of the time there is enough natural humidity in the greenhouse to take care of their slight need. In fact, during dull fall weather, it may be necessary to open the ventilators and turn on the heat to expel the heavy dampness.

The resting season is just the opposite with African and South American varieties which include mesembryanthemum, lithops, and most of the crassula. They are summer-dormant and do most of their growing in winter. It is a good idea to separate these classes for simplicity of handling.

None of the succulents want much fertilizer, for their fine roots can easily be burned. Weak applications of a complete liquid fertilizer which includes the trace elements is helpful to mature plants during the growing season.

April or September is the time to repot, though March and May are satisfactory. Disturbing the roots during any other season should be done only in emergencies. Small plants may need a size larger pot each year, but mature plants can go two or three years without repotting. Place broken crock in the bottom of the pot, up to as much as halfway, and press the new soil firmly around the root ball, but do not pack hard.

From May to October, plants can be set out of doors where air can circulate freely around them. A roof built of several 3- by 6-foot sections of hot-bed sash on a frame of two-by-fours gives excellent protection against heavy rains. Slats can be placed around the sides during cooler weather, and in the hot summer the glass can easily be shaded to exclude about fifty per cent of the light.

15

Vegetables and Fruits

IMAGINE THE THRILL of stepping into your greenhouse to pick a crisp head of lettuce, some luscious sunripened tomatoes, and a fresh bunch of radishes when it is freezing outdoors. Even though you may not have much space, it is grand to grow a few vegetables for their fresh flavor.

Practically any vegetable can be grown under glass. I have even seen home-greenhouse crops of corn and cabbage, but now with fast transportation from the South, and fresh vegetables so readily available and inexpensive, even commercial greenhouse men have difficulty in making the most adaptable crops pay.

Fruits such as grapes, nectarines, peaches, lemons, and pears, were also once popular in estate greenhouses. They were espaliered or grown as dwarf trees at high cost. You still see a few in some show places, but they are not for the small home greenhouse.

The compact-growing vegetables that yield well in a small space are worth while. Parsley, scallions, radishes, lettuce, mint, chives, and almost all of the herbs are a good choice. If your greenhouse is large, you will also enjoy tomatoes, Swiss chard, carrots, and beets.

Out-of-season strawberries are especially delicious, but there are never enough. Melons and cucumbers are outstanding, too, but the space needed is out of all proportion to the value of the yield, unless these are grown as a summer crop in a greenhouse that would otherwise be empty.

The rich, friable soil that is so good for general greenhouse crops as described in Chapter 6 is also excellent for vegetables. In some cases, the addition of a liberal amount of sharp sand is beneficial, as pointed out in the directions for individual crops.

Most vegetables want all the sun they can get. They are particularly heavy feeders when the weather is bright, and at these times they may be fed with applications of fertilizer such as manure water, nitrate of soda, ammonium sulfate, or one of the quick-acting liquid fertilizers.

Vegetables require a good supply of moisture evenly distributed from the top to the bottom of the bed, and they do well in a humid atmosphere. For good quality and quantity yield, keep them growing along rapidly from seed germination to maturity. If plants become hard through a check at any stage of their growth, they seldom recover, and you may as well discard them and start anew.

Radishes

Radishes are an easy crop in the greenhouse, just as they are out of doors. The small globe varieties are the best. Seed sown from early October on, with subsequent sowings about every three to four weeks, insures a constant supply.

Radishes grown in a light, sandy soil are smoother, more uniform in size, and more tender than when grown in heavy soil. Grow in 5- or 6-inch-deep flats or benches. Sow about twenty seeds to the foot, in rows 4 to 5 inches apart. When they are up, thin to eight or ten plants to the foot. Radishes grow larger and mature more rapidly if given ample space. When most of the radishes are pulled, another sowing can be made between rows.

Grow cool—45° at night; ten degrees higher during the daytime.

Lettuce

Sow lettuce about the end of August and make successive sowings every fifteen to twenty days throughout the winter. Sow seeds thinly, and transplant after three weeks to avoid damping-off. Set the plants 6 to 8 inches apart in the bench, taking as much soil as possible on the roots. Shade with newspaper for a day or two. Lettuce likes lots of water, so do not be too sparing with it. Perhaps that is why this crop does particularly well when grown by the automatic watering culture methods without soil. See Chapter 20.

Keep the plants growing continually for the best quality and largest heads. Try White Boston, May King, Boston Market, Matchless, or Butternut for head lettuce. Grand Rapids or Oak Leaf make good loose heads.

Cauliflower

If you were to ask which vegetable is the most satisfying to grow in a moderate-size greenhouse, the answer would be *cauliflower*. Big heads of tender texture are easily grown. Sow seeds September 15 for heads in late December or January. Transplant seedlings early into 3-inch pots or plant bands. Bench about 15 inches apart when a heavy root system has formed. Soil should be at least 6 inches deep; 8 inches is preferable for good distribution of moisture is important. Water plants well when benching, and then keep soil evenly moist from top to bottom. Water on the foliage does no harm before heads begin to form, but must be avoided thereafter.

The optimum night temperature for cauliflower is 50 to 55°, but they do well at 45 to 50°. Daytime temperature may be 60 to 70°. This crop is very sensitive to drafts, so use care with ventilation.

When heads are about 2 inches in diameter, they must have protection to keep them white, otherwise the heads turn brown and become coarser in texture. In the greenhouse, a double thickness of brown paper spread over the top gives the best protection, though the cauliflower leaves may be tied with string or rubber bands in the usual way used outdoors.

Tomatoes

While tomatoes are a warm crop (72°) and require a good deal of space, many find it profitable to grow a few plants in small greenhouses. Seeds for the first are sown about July 1st, because fruit must be set before the cloudy weather and short days of fall arrive. Such a crop will mature in late October even in a moderate-temperature greenhouse (55°) and will continue profitably until January. The second crop is started in January; plants are benched in March and bear fruit in June.

It is possible to propagate plants from cuttings, but they are never as productive as those raised from seed.

Shift the young plants twice for husky growth before benching. First to a flat, about 2 inches apart. Next, to 3-inch pots or veneer plant bands. Never let plants stop growing or become hard and pot-bound.

Bench tomato plants about 18 inches apart or grow in 10- to 12-inch pots. Keep plants pruned to one or two stems; when more remain, maturity is slow. Some of the leaves may be trimmed, too, if growth becomes rank. Stake the plants, or run soft rope down from wires strung horizontally along the roof. Twine the plants around the supports and tie with soft string or "Twist-ems." The top of the plants may be pinched off when they reach the roof of the greenhouse. A mulch of manure or peat moss will help to keep moisture in the soil. Tomatoes want a lot of moisture but not so much as to promote excessive leaf growth.

Pollenization by hand is necessary when blossoms appear. Shake the vines periodically to float the fine pollen into the air. Another method that is more certain but more trouble is to collect pollen by shaking it onto a magnifying glass and pollenizing the blossoms with a camel's-hair brush.

Plant only the early varieties for winter forcing. The later ones take too long to mature. My favorites are still Bonny Best (red) and John Baer (red), but any of the good early varieties are suitable.

Beets

Grow beets both for the greens and the roots. Sow seeds directly in the bench in drills 10 inches apart. Thin to from 2 to 3 inches. The night temperature may be from 45 to 50°. Early varieties are best for forcing.

Carrots

Use the early, short-horn type carrots for forcing. Sow seeds in rows 6 inches apart, and thin to 2 inches apart. A light soil with plenty of sharp sand promotes smooth, uniform roots, just as with radishes. Bottom heat is needed for forcing in midwinter, but carrots can be grown as a spring crop without it.

Swiss Chard

Here's a good crop that produces throughout the entire winter. Raise any variety of Swiss chard you like in the same manner as lettuce. The large seed may be sown directly in the bench and thinned out about 2 to 4 inches apart, or they may be started in flats first and then benched. Don't bother with moving plants from the outdoor garden into the greenhouse, for chard is so easily grown from seed, and new plants always yield more than old.

Parsley

Both curly and flat-leaf parsley is suited to forcing. Plants may be raised easily from seed in the fall and set in rows about 6 inches apart or grown in pots which can be brought indoors for use as required. Parsley from outdoors can be cut back during the fall and the roots planted in the greenhouse where they soon develop new growth; but do not try to grow the same plants a second year for they just go to seed.

Melons and Cucumbers

These two crops require a high temperature and considerable headroom, so it is not likely you will want to raise them during the winter. As an early summer crop, it is a different story. If seeds are sown March 1st, four to six weeks may be gained over outdoor crops with much better results.

Sow seeds in plant bands or pots to avoid harming tender roots in transplanting. Set plants 18 to 24 inches apart in light, sandy soil. Keep vines pruned to a single stem, and train them on stakes or heavy cord extending from wires strung horizontally along the roof of the greenhouse. These crops want lots of sunlight and can be grown close to the glass right up to the peak of the roof. Melons require a night temperature of 70 to 75°; cucumbers—65°.

Hand pollenization with a camel's-hair brush from male to female flowers may be necessary if there are no bees to enter the greenhouse. Another thing with melons, never leave the greenhouse door open because rats are fond of the seed. I once lost every melon in a beautiful crop this way, just when the fruit was ready to pick.

Melons for forcing include Golden Beauty with pink flesh, Pink Flesh, and King George with red flesh, and Royal Jubilee with green flesh. The Persians do well too.

Good greenhouse varieties of cucumbers are White Spine and Telegraph.

Asparagus and Rhubarb

These two vegetables may be grown without difficulty during the winter and only occupy bench space a short time. You can crowd the roots to a fare-thee-well, yet produce a crop far more tender and superior to any outdoor kind. Dig the roots during the fall, and store them in a pit or unheated shed where they will freeze and get a resting period. Cover with hay and soil so they will not dry out. Plant in boxes, whenever you choose during the winter, deep enough to provide an inch of soil on top and 2 inches underneath. For bleached asparagus, cover with 6 to 8 inches of soil.

Place the boxes under the benches until growth is so high they must be moved. Large, three- to four-year-old roots are best, but older ones may be used.

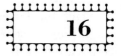

16

Growing Plants From Seed

ONE OF THE MOST enjoyable and profitable green-house operations is raising plants from seed. You can grow them by the thousands in a comparatively small amount of space to have all you want for your outdoor and indoor garden. You don't have to be satisfied with run-of-the-mill varieties either, for you can have all the improved introductions, novelties, and hybrids, as soon as seeds are available, and you can even grow your very own hybrids. The quality of plants grown from seed is better, or at least you find it so, for no flowers or vegetables are quite so satisfying as those you raise yourself.

Good growth is practically assured in the greenhouse, since all controlling influences are as perfect as can be; you have only to take sanitary precautions to prevent damp-off—see Chapter 19; control the soil moisture, light, and ventilation to raise the healthiest of plants.

Except for superphosphate, fertilizers should not be added to compost used for planting seeds. The seeds carry enough within themselves to get started. Small seeds carry less than large ones, but even they should get enough from the compost to grow up to transplanting size. If soil is lacking in phosphorous, superphosphate may be mixed in at the rate of a 3-inch potful to a bushel of soil.

Compost

Nearly every experienced old-timer you meet, likes to use soil mixture for starting his seed. He takes one-third composted soil, as described in Chapter 6, and adds one-third granulated peat moss and one-third clean, sharp sand. Nowadays, many prefer to screen in dried sphagnum moss, vermiculite, or perlite instead of the peat moss, because these materials are sterile and never become soggy, but any of them will give good results.

Never use soil straight from the garden, unless it is from a spot that has had plenty of manure or other humus-making material worked into it the season before. If this has not been done, the soil will soon become compressed and the much-needed oxygen will be shut out.

It always pays to use precautions. Sterilize your soil by one of the methods explained in Chapter 6 or use one of the sterile seed-sowing media which retains a constant and even supply of moisture over a long period yet is sufficiently light and aerated to furnish oxygen to the roots. To have these qualities the material must be light and porous and must not become hard or crusty on the surface.

Other Media

Instead of a soil mixture, straight vermiculite, sand, sphagnum moss, or peat moss are frequently used for starting seed. The vermiculite should be of the medium or fine grade. Sand must be the coarse, sharp kind from a pit or quarry; seashore sand packs hard and becomes crusty. Wash the pit or quarry sand in a pail, box, or barrel, continually stirring it as you flush with the hose. Perlite, a sterile, volcanic glass rock which helps drainage, is a good substitute for sand. Dried sphagnum moss must be rubbed through a ¼-inch-mesh screen and wet down several times with a fine sprinkle to get it evenly moist. It holds water for longer periods than most media.

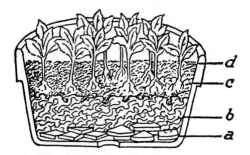

Seedlings. Cross-section sketch of bulb pan, showing (a) broken crock (b) sphagnum moss (c) soil (d) thin layer of sphagnum moss or sand.

The peat moss you get is usually acid, though neutral peat moss is available. The acid is not a drawback with most plants, however, because they are in the media so short a time. Many prefer it mixed half-and-half with sand both for starting seed and rooting cuttings. Sand alone dries out fast and needs too much attention.

Planting

Seed flats, shallow clay bulb-pans, pots, and sometimes tin cans with holes punched in the bottom to permit drainage, are used for starting seeds. When seed flats are used, a layer of sphagnum moss, wood slats, pieces of shingle, or ½-inch of gravel is placed in the bottom to prevent the soil from washing through. Pieces of broken pots or small stones are used with pans, pots, or cans to provide drainage.

The flat or pot is filled heaping with the compost or other medium used and leveled off with a stick as shown in the photograph. Then the air spaces are dispelled by striking the bottom several times on a work table.

Next the surface is tamped with a small block. Press down firmly, but do not pack. This is important with all media. If compost is used, a layer of clean sand, sphagnum moss, vermiculite or perlite may be sieved over the surface, wet down with a fine spray, and tamped as before.

Then the seeds are planted. If fine, they are broadcast on the surface and tamped down. No further covering is wanted. If they are larger, they are sown in rows about 2 inches apart. All seeds should be carefully labeled at the time of planting because it is difficult to distinguish young plants in their first growth.

A covering to the depth of about twice the size of the seed is about right for most varieties. This covering can be spread on through a fine sieve. After planting, the seeds are watered well. Take care to use a light, fine spray from a bulb, a spray head on a hose, or a rose on a watering can. If a hose or watering can is used, first test the force of spray on the walk before bringing it over to the flat so there will be no washout.

Better than surface watering is subirrigation. This may be accomplished by placing the container in a pan containing an inch or two of water and allowing it to draw up its own moisture through the drainage holes in the bottom by capillary attraction. One good watering in the beginning should be enough until the seeds have germinated, but the surface of the soil must never be allowed to dry out.

After watering, a covering placed over the top of the seed flat or pot cuts down evaporation and maintains a steady temperature. A piece of glass, paper, or burlap is generally used. If glass is used, sieve a fine covering of sand over the surface of the glass for shade. During warm, sunny weather, burlap soaked in water makes the best covering.

The temperature should be maintained as evenly as possible. Sudden changes and drafts cause conditions that promote damping-off. A glassed-over propagating bed with electric, soil-heating cable is ideal for starting tender seedlings. A temperature of 65° is about right for most of the hardier plants such as snapdragons, cabbage, and lettuce. Seventy to 75° is wanted for the more tender plants such as eggplant, melons, petunias, and coleus. As a general rule, a temperature ten degrees higher than the one at which the plant is regularly grown is about right for starting the seed, but cyclamen and cineraria like a cool germinating temperature of about 50°.

Thinning Out

As soon as the seeds have germinated, the glass, paper, or burlap covering is removed. This is the time to make sure plants do not become checked, grow leggy, or damp-off.

When the seedlings are large enough, thin out to admit light and a free circulation of air. Tweezers may be needed if the plants are too tiny to handle with your fingers. If pulling disturbs the roots of all the seedlings, merely pinch off the weakest plants close to the soil.

Transplanting

Transplant just as soon as the seedlings are large enough to handle. This will be when the true leaves appear. Crowding is never desirable, since sunlight as well as fresh air is needed. It is far better to have a few hundred good, healthy plants than a thousand leggy, weak ones.

Seedlings take transplanting much better when they are small than when larger. Moving them is bound to break off fine roots, but many new ones branch out and make a more vigorous root system. Transplant the seedlings into 2½-inch pots or seed flats. The soil must be fine, aerated, and rich in humus to produce stocky plants. About one-third peat moss may be mixed in to make up for any humus deficiency, along with super-phosphate at the rate of a 3-inch potful to a bushel of soil. If you don't have good compost of your own, buy some from your local florist rather than take chances on ordinary garden soil.

If the plants are to be transplanted into seed flats, a board to spot the holes in which to set the plants makes the job go faster. The prongs of a discarded wooden rake would make a good spotting-board if available. The spots in mine are spaced about 1½ inches apart. For larger plants, every other space is used instead of every one. A bluntly pointed plastic dibble that you can buy, or a hardwood one that you can make yourself, is helpful in enlarging the holes and in pressing the soil firmly around the roots.

Gentle handling is always a *must* in transplanting.

Speed is secondary to good results and this means having everything prepared beforehand—the soil in clean flats or pots, a good place to work, and the few necessary tools.

Jogging the edges of the flat or pot in which the seedlings have been grown, against the work bench, makes it possible to lift them more easily. It makes the soil separate from the edges so you can get at them. The seedlings can be kept on the dry side for a week before transplanting to harden them for the shock, but always water just beforehand, so as much soil as possible clings to the roots.

The roots should never be bent or doubled under in transplanting, but should be suspended into the hole. The soil is pressed firmly about them by pushing the dibble into it all around the seedling. Then water to make soil cling to the roots. Water carefully though. Just as when starting seeds, it is best to subirrigate by setting the pot or flat in a larger tray of water and letting it draw up its own moisture.

Feeding with liquid fertilizer may be started when the plants have taken hold. For a quick boost, I like ammonium sulfate or nitrate of soda mixed one level tablespoon to two gallons of water. Use nitrate of soda if your soil is acid and ammonium sulfate if it is alkaline. Applications may be made about every two weeks.

A miniature cultivator is a very handy tool to have on hand. You can make one yourself by bending wire, see page 45, and using it to break any crust which may form on the surface of the soil. This will help to aerate the soil, and keep it free of weeds. If you take the trouble to set the plants in even rows, it is easy to cultivate in both directions.

Plant bands of wood veneer or building paper are excellent for transplanting. Additional nitrogenous fertilizer is needed with wood bands to make up for that which decomposition robs from the soil. Clay pots are good but take much more space and require more attention since they dry out faster.

17

Growing Plants From Cuttings

ONCE YOU DISCOVER how easily you can reproduce new plants from cuttings taken from your old ones, you will be multiplying all the plants you can lay your hands on. That is, you will do so unless you are different from most of us who garden under glass.

At the start, it may be the easy-to-root plants such as ivy, geraniums, chrysanthemums, and phlox which take your attention. Next, it may be camellias, hibiscus, roses, holly, and similar ornamental plants. After that, you'll be casting a covetous eye about the gardens of friends and neighbors to beg slips of plants you don't have in your own. The rooting of cuttings is so alluring that no plant which strikes your fancy will be safe.

Cuttings taken from growth that is strong, healthy, and vigorous have the best chance of making good plants. Remember your cutting has no roots and must have ability to take up water, plus the stamina to resist rot until the new roots have formed.

Select half mature growth from terminal branches.

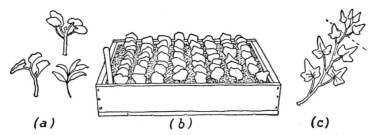

Cuttings. (a) Terminal cuttings (b) leaf cuttings (c) vine cuttings.

Older growth is so hard that there is not enough activity in the root-making tissues of the cutting; new growth is unsatisfactory because it is too soft and lacks the energy reserve. Vine cuttings should not be from the terminal ends, but back two or three nodes or joints. The end growth is usually too soft.

The length of the cutting depends upon the variety of plant. It may vary from 2 to 6 inches, but should have from three to six leaves. The longer the cutting, the faster you have good plants, but it must be able to absorb enough moisture to make up for the amount transpired through the leaves.

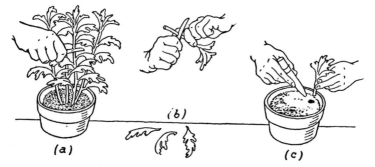

Cuttings. (a) Selecting the cuttings (b) making the cut (c) planting.

A sharp knife is needed, as the cut must be clean and straight across, without bruising the tissue. A smooth cut heals much faster than a jagged one made by breaking off the slips. Make the cut at a node or just a little below one where growth is of the right maturity. Strip the leaves off at the base of the cutting and plant as soon as possible.

Root growth may be stimulated by the use of root-promoting substances containing plant hormones. These are available in both liquid and powdered form. They not only speed up the time of rooting, but induce a greater amount of roots to grow and make it possible to root cuttings that ordinarily do not take easily. The usual method is to dust the end of the cutting with powder or let it stand for the required time in the liquid. Any surplus powder or liquid is shaken off before planting.

The cuttings may be planted in seed flats, bulb pans, pots, or a propagating bench. The bench need not be a special one or very large one. About 3 feet of a regular 2½-foot-wide growing bench should be large enough, for cuttings may be set closely together. It can be divided from the rest of the bench with boards, and the drainage cracks may be covered up with slats, coarse gravel, or sphagnum moss.

The Media

Vermiculite, which is composed of expanded mica pellets, is now replacing sand as the most popular rooting medium. It is sterile and holds large quantities of moisture evenly over a long period. Planting is easier, for you merely have to press the cutting in, and the particles cling to it without pounding as with sand. In fact, vermiculite packs solid if you tamp it too hard. Simply insert the cutting and press the vermiculite around it with your fingers.

Vermiculite comes in fine, medium, and coarse grades. The coarse grade has worked out more successfully than the others for me and several specialists have expressed the same preference. Perhaps the coarse particles allow a greater movement of oxygen.

Sand is still the most popular medium with professional gardeners, I think simply because they spent much time learning how to use it. You can use it straight or mixed with one-third peat moss or sphagnum moss. Many African violet growers say there is nothing better than sand and dried sphagnum moss. Be sure the sand you use is coarse and sharp. Never use it without first flushing it clean with a hose.

Planting

Smooth the medium with a block of wood and stick the cuttings in straight rows with enough space between them to allow a free circulation of air. If sand is the medium used, make a hole with a dibble first or you will damage the root-making tissues.

Water thoroughly right after planting, and continue to provide adequate moisture, and add to the humidity by shading. In spring and summer, syringe cuttings to reduce transpiration of moisture through the leaves. Hot, dry air increases transpiration, which is detrimental since cuttings have no roots to take in water. Keep the medium moderately moist at all times. Watering once a week should be adequate in winter and dull weather, but more will be needed in summer. Shade well with newspaper the first few days to reduce evaporation, and then partially shade with cheesecloth or slats.

The humidity and temperature surrounding the cuttings can be controlled more effectively by having a sash with shaded glass hinged to the propagating bench. This is almost essential with plants that are difficult to root.

Propagation bench.

Bottom heat is a great aid to rooting most cuttings, especially woody kinds, and it is easily provided by means of a plastic- or lead-covered heating cable. Use a good soil thermometer. Sixty-five to 75° is about the right temperature for rooting most plants.

Leaf Cuttings

This method of reproduction is widely used with African violets (see page 90) and also such plants as ornamental begonias and peperomias. With large-leaved plants, ½-inch or more can be cut away from the outside edge to lessen the rate of transpiration. Roots form where the veins are injured, so cut out small sections across the veins. These leaves are then laid in a rooting medium, as described above, and lightly covered. They will require staking down with hairpins or wire staples to keep them in close contact with the medium. New plants grow at the cuts. Another method is to cut the edges off the leaves until they are about one-third the original size, bringing the base containing the central vein down to a point and planting the point in the medium. Smaller-leaved plants, such as African violets, may be rooted easily by merely inserting the stems ½ inch, into the medium.

High humidity, such as provided in a glass-covered bench, is helpful. When the young plants appear, they may be fed with weak liquid fertilizer. Allow them to become well-established before transplanting.

Root Cuttings

Sections of roots and segments of bulbs or corms are easily rooted in vermiculite or sand. Start them in early spring just as new growth begins. Make the cut with a sharp knife, and include two or more shoots or leaves with each segment. Daffodils, clivia, dahlias, cyclamen, gloxinias, and almost all fleshy-rooted plants can be multiplied this way.

Transplanting

Dig up one or two cuttings and examine them as soon as you think roots have formed. Darkening of the leaves is an indication that growth has started. Transplant into soil as soon as roots are ½ to 1 inch long. Do not let them stay in the propagating bed any longer or they will become starved and stunted. Keep the plants shaded after potting and syringe occasionally to reduce transpiration. Follow the same procedure for potting and planting as described in Chapter 18.

18

The Knack of Potting

Good drainage and aeration is the big thing for success with potted plants. Use a soil that is lighter and looser than you would for plants in benches. A soil mixture consisting of three parts composted sod, one part sand and one part peat moss or leaf mold is satisfactory for general purposes.

The amount of moisture required by a particular plant variety can be controlled by the soil mixture. Additional sand can be added for plants which should be kept on the dry side, such as many cacti and succulents, or leaf mold may be increased up to two parts for finely rooted plants such as begonias, calceolaria, and primroses.

Plants in the early stages of growth (small rooted-cuttings and seedlings) want a soil that is made up of finer particles to start with, than they do later on. In potting them up for the first time, use 2½ or 3-inch pots; plants in smaller-size pots are too difficult for the beginner to take care of. Run the soil through a sieve of about ¼-inch-mesh wire.

181

After the plants have become established and are ready to go into 4-inch and larger-size pots, they need a coarser soil. Most soils are deficient in phosphorous so superphosphate or a complete fertilizer such as 4-12-4 should be added beforehand at the rate of a 3-inch pot to a bushel of soil. Do not sieve the soil, merely make it friable by working it with a spade.

Some professional gardeners and florists use the famous Merton's potting-compost formula for all their pot plants, and sing loudly in its praise. It was developed by the John Innes Institute of Horticultural Research near London. I have been told that at Kew Gardens it is used most extensively. Anyone wishing to take the little extra time to mix a supply may find it well worth the trouble. Take seven parts loam, three parts of peat moss, two of sand, and to each bushel mix one-and-a-half ounces of horn meal, one-and-a-half ounces of superphosphate, three-quarter ounce of ground limestone, and three-quarter ounce of muriate of potash.

The first step to successful and speedy potting is to arrange conveniently all the materials, such as pots, soil, and plants, on the potting bench beforehand. Pots must be clean; those that have been used previously should be washed in warm water. Soaking will soften the algae and other deposits that cling to them. Soak new pots in water so that they will not draw the moisture out of the soil, but allow them to drain for about an hour before use. Soil clings to wet or dirty pots and breaks the root ball when you are repotting.

Small seedlings and rooted cuttings should be potted before they become too large or starved. Seedlings may be transplanted as soon as their first true leaves are established; cuttings are moved when the roots are ½ to

1 inch long. The earlier the young plants are moved, the less chance of damp-off. The soil or sand in which they grew should be fairly moist before the plants are lifted so that some of the medium clings to the roots and the plants will take hold with minimum set-back.

Be gentle—use your first finger or a plant-tag to lift the young plants. Line the pots up on the potting table and fill them to the top with moderately moist soil. Dry soil

Potting young seedlings.

will damage the young roots. A small amount of drainage material such as fine crock, gravel or charcoal may be placed in the bottom, but this is not necessary in pots under 4 inches. Make a hole in the center of the soil with your finger; place the root in it and press the soil down firmly but gently all around the stem. Soil around rooted cuttings and young plants should be firm but not hard-packed. The plants may be set deeper in the soil than they originally grew, usually up to the first leaves. Fill the small pot to about ¼ inch from the top so there will be room for water.

Water gently right after potting. Subirrigation by placing the pots in a shallow pan, containing about ½ inch of water, where they can draw up moisture through the drainage hole, is the safest method.

Plunging the potted plants in damp sand or cinders helps to keep them moist and prevents them from toppling over. Shade with paper or with cheesecloth stretched over wires above the bench for about three to five days, depending upon the season. After the plants have made good growth and just before they become pot-bound, shift them to their next place of growth, either in a bench or into larger pots. Never allow them to become root-bound or they will become hard, starved, and stunted. Knock one of the plants out of its pot occasionally to examine the condition of the roots.

When you want to remove a plant from its pot, place your hand over the pot with first and second finger on each side of the stem to hold the soil. Invert the pot and give the rim a sharp rap on the edge of the bench. Do not try to remove a plant when the soil is dried out—water well first and let drain for a half-hour so the root ball will remain intact.

When the roots have started to crowd and require more room, transfer the plants to pots just one or two sizes larger so it won't take long for them to grow out into the fresh soil. Overpotting leaves a thick ring of soil around the outside of the root ball that becomes so soggy and compressed the roots don't have much of a chance. It is only in porous, well-aerated soil that plants can prosper.

When transferring a plant to a larger pot, place some broken crock, coarse gravel, or charcoal over the drainage hole to keep it open. In very large pots a covering of sphagnum moss on top of the drainage material is also helpful to keep it clean. Place a small amount of soil in the bottom of the pot, remembering that the root ball should come up to about half an inch from the top when you finish. Next, hold the plant in the center of the pot with the left hand, scoop some soil up with the right, and pour it all around the edge. Then take the pot in both hands and give the bottom a sharp rap or two on

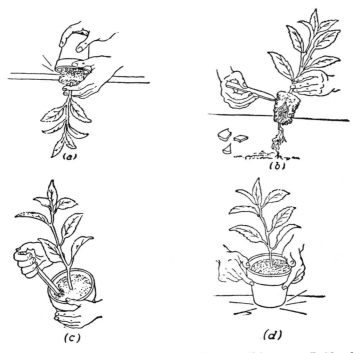

Repotting Old Plants. (a) Remove plant from pot (b) scrape off old soil and dead roots (c) work new soil firmly around the root ball (d) rap the pot to exclude free air spaces.

the bench to firm the soil. Work the soil down in with your fingers and again give the pot a sharp rap on the bench. Water immediately after repotting.

Repotting Ornamental Plants

Flowering and foliage plants that live in pots or tubs year after year will need repotting or top-dressing periodically to renew the soil. Some will need to go into larger pots, others can go back in the same pots, and still others will need smaller ones. An examination of the roots will soon tell. Fall or late spring, after the plants have finished flowering or are just starting new growth, is the best time. Plants showing roots that are white and alive should be shifted to larger pots, but if the roots are a massed network of yellow and brown they are not live roots and can be scraped loose with a wooden plant tag along with some of the old soil. Then, depending upon the size of the ball, the plant can go back into its original pot or into a smaller one.

Be sure that the root ball is well moistened right to the center before repotting, and press the new soil firmly against the roots. If the plant is large, do not try to save the old pot or tub; it is better to break it so the plant won't be damaged. Use very coarse, loose soil for the big plants, working in a little soil at a time. Push it down firmly with a stick; a piece of lath will do, or you can easily make a potting stick. See page 45. Force can be used in repotting woody, dormant plants, but care is needed with more tender varieties.

A top-dressing with fresh soil is in order with large plants in the years when you do not repot. Simply scoop away some of the old soil from the surface and down around the rim of the pot, being careful not to disturb the roots. Work in fresh soil and tamp with a potting stick.

19

Pest and Disease Control

I T'S EASY TO KEEP your plants free of pests in a green-house—much easier than in the outdoor garden. You discover this very quickly when your greenhouse is new. Plants thrive so well in the clean atmosphere and fresh soil that you get the idea there never will be any trouble. At least that's the way it was with me.

Then, after four or six weeks, I noticed some little white flies around a cineraria gift plant, white fuzz on the stems of coleus, and small spaces in the tissue of chrysanthemum leaves. A friend who majored in ento-mology also pointed out some scars on the leaves of snap-dragons. "You've got thrips, too," he said. Then, as I read about all the different kinds of insects and diseases you *could have* and how rapidly they spread, it seemed almost impossible to grow anything well.

I fumigated with tobacco stems, sprayed with nicotine sulfate, and dusted with tobacco dust. The thrips and midge vanished, but the white fly and mealy bug lingered on.

Finally with much bravado, I fumigated with the deadly poisonous, calcium cyanide and cleaned them out, too. It was all so simple. Fortunately, only one good bug killer is needed to do the whole job today. It is safe, too, and need only be used about once every two weeks. But before going into this and other controls, let's learn to recognize the insects and diseases you are most likely to meet in the greenhouse.

Aphids. The most common insects in the greenhouse are green and black aphids or plant lice. There are many types of these insects. Some are slightly larger than others, but all have the same general appearance.

They attack nearly everything in the greenhouse, just as they do in the outdoor garden. The small, sucking insects multiply so rapidly, that if left unchecked, they literally cover the plants and draw the very life out of them. Each aphid grows to maturity in about twelve days and reproduces a new generation of thirty to thirty-five at a time. When one plant becomes overcrowded with the lice, some of them will form wings and fly to another plant. Ants transport them also. Black aphids infest nearly all plants. Green flies are found on tulips, lilies, iris, primroses, snapdragons, calendula, roses, carnations, and other plants.

Midge. While midge is a small fly, your introduction to it is usually in the form of numerous tiny galls underneath the tissues of chrysanthemum leaves. These look like little bumps or raised specks and are a result of the eggs laid by the adult fly. The fly punctures the epidermis and lays the eggs; the eggs hatch into larvae and continue to remain in the cell; the pupa forms and soon emerges as a fly. The time for all this is fifty days.

Mealy Bug. The mealy bug looks like a dab of white

cotton. It primarily infests begonias, geraniums, gardenias, amaryllis, and chrysanthemums. It is very difficult to control with sprays, because the cottony covering is waxy and highly protective.

Red Spider Mite. Red spider infests many plants in the greenhouse. It is not always easy to detect because it is sometimes yellow and green, and usually so small that it cannot be seen with the naked eye, but the work that it does can easily be detected. The foliage of infested plants takes on a grayish color and is mottled in appearance. The mites attack the underside of leaves, especially the young, tender ones. They suck out the juices, and seem to thrive under dry conditions. Almost all greenhouse plants and vegetables are susceptible to them, especially roses, carnations, peas, snapdragons, chrysanthemums, and asters.

Cyclamen Mites mostly attack the tender young shoots of cyclamen, begonias, delphinium, African violets, gloxinias and other gesneriads. They distort the foliage and cause it to turn black.

Leaf Tier or Rollers. These are green or bronze caterpillars that fasten leaves together with a web. They are not prevalent, but can attack practically all greenhouse crops. You'll know they are present when you see leaves rolled up or tucked under and filled with ragged holes. They are easy to exterminate and should be destroyed.

Scale. These are sucking insects which attach themselves tightly to the foliage and stems of cacti and succulents, palms, ferns, ivies, poinsettias, and shrubs having smooth bark. They are oval-shaped and appear as crusty brown scabs when mature.

Thrips. Thrips are so small you have to use a magnifying glass to detect them. They are yellowish brown in color, very thin, and have narrow wings. Leaves injured by their rasping of tissues and the sucking out of the juices take on a silvery appearance. They attack asters, chrysanthemums, cineraria, calceolaria, narcissus, roses, snapdragons, carnations, primroses, sweet peas, gladiolus, geraniums and many other greenhouse plants.

White Fly. When you meet this pest of pests you have little trouble in detecting it. In no time, thousands collect on the undersides of leaves. It is not hard to kill the minute, white moths with sprays and dusts, but the day after you think you've killed them all, there seem to be more than ever. The eggs that the fly lays on the undersides of leaves keep on developing into nymphs, and the nymphs remain there, sucking the juices out of the plants as though nothing had happened. Sprays will not touch their waxy coats. They like geraniums, lantana, gerbera, cineraria, calceolaria, and especially ageratum, tomatoes and cucumbers.

All-Purpose Spray

Here's a one shot spray that will keep your greenhouse free of all the usual pests and diseases. It was developed and tested by our leading entomologists and pathologists at agricultural colleges and has been successfully used by commercial operators, as well as home greenhouse gardeners. The malathion is particularly effective and the DDT gives it extra punch, especially against the chewing insects.

To one gallon of water add:

2 level tablespoons of 25 per cent malathion wettable powder

1 level tablespoon of zineb

1 level tablespoon wettable sulfur (when needed)

1 level tablespoon of DDT 50 per cent wettable powder

1 level teaspoon of Dreft as a spreader

The concentration of the spray is not strong so it will not harm even the most tender plants. The residue stays on the foliage and continues to kill for a week or more, but to protect the new growth as well, spray every ten days to two weeks.

All the ingredients needed to make this spray are available from the larger garden suppliers. The malathion kills mealy bug, white fly, red spider, aphids, scale, thrips, and many others. The DDT gives it extra kick for killing most insects except aphids and red spider.

A number of insecticides and dusts are made especially for one particular hard-to-kill group of pests. Some of the best are the following: *Dimite,* available from Acme Quality Paint Co. in Detroit, and effective against red spider mite, but not insects; *Aramite 15-W* made by the U.S. Rubber Co. in Bethany, Conn., also a very effective miticide with little or no effect on insects; *Lindane,* available in most garden supply stores, does a job on aphids, leaf miners, and midge.

Of course, it is possible to buy highly effective brand-name insecticide-fungicide combinations that contain these or similar ingredients. Some of the most popular are:

> End-O-Pest Rose Dust
> End-O-Pest Rose Spray
> J & P Rose Dust
> J & P Rose Spray
> A.C.P. Rose and Floral Dust

Protexall Garden Spray
DuPont All Purpose Rose Spray
Tri-ogen Rose Dust
Tri-ogen Rose Spray

While malathion, DDT, and others mentioned are among the safest insecticides now available, they are poisonous and should be used with respect in the confines of a small greenhouse. In fact, they are not as poisonous as the familiar nicotine sulfate but are poisonous even if swallowed in a diluted form. So take the following precautions:

(1) Avoid prolonged breathing of the mist and especially the concentrated powder when mixing.

(2) Keep materials out of reach of small children and avoid contamination of food or foodstuff.

A respirator is not necessary, but it is always a good idea to leave the ventilators open while spraying and for five or ten minutes afterward.

Fumigants

It is much easier to fumigate than spray. If your greenhouse is free-standing or connected to a building where entering fumes will not matter, you can fumigate with smoke generators that do an excellent job. I have had particularly good success with one containing dithio known as Plantfume 103-A. It is put up by the Plant Products Co. of Blue Point, N.Y. The smallest sizes are for 2,000 cubic feet but if your greenhouse is smaller, it is a simple matter to measure out the right proportion. Sparklers provide the fuse to ignite the fumigant. You light them near the handle, insert the top end into the powder and are well on your way out before the smoke begins to pour forth.

Other excellent fumigators are made by the Fulex Co. of Woburn, Mass. There is a good general-purpose bug killer containing parathion, one for resistant red spider mites, and one that is especially good for aphids is also effective on many other bugs. I have used all of these fumigants in my greatly varied group of plants without any damage whatsoever. In fact, if anything, the recommended concentrations of the majority are a bit on the safe side.

If your greenhouse is connected to your house, it would be unsafe to use such fumigants. Even sealing the door or other openings with tape will not keep out the fumes. This, however, does not keep some owners of attached greenhouses, including garden editor, Fred Rockwell, from using fumigants. Fred's beautiful lean-to greenhouse at West Nyack, N.Y., leads right off the dining room, but he uses the fumigants when no one will be home for the night.

Other Pests

Nematodes. Root-knot nematodes are tiny eel worms that bore into the roots of plants causing galls to form on them. Badly infested plants become stunted, and while they do not die, they never amount to much. Foliar nematodes feed on the leaves of begonias and chrysanthemums. Their damage can be detected by brownish spots and deformation of the lower foliage. Soil sterilization with Larvacide or Dowfume MC-2, Soilfume Caps, Bromofume or Shell D-D (See Chapter 6) are effective controls for root knot. Wash benches and spray underneath them with formaldehyde, mixed 1 to 50. Foliar nematode can be completely controlled by keeping the foliage dry.

Snails and Slugs. These pests are most apt to be a nuisance in greenhouses where it is necessary to maintain a high humidity, such as in an orchid house. Slug-baits containing methaldehyde, many of which are on the market, give almost perfect control. Picking these pests by hand or with a pair of tweezers, if you prefer, is another way of getting rid of them. They can most easily be collected at night by flashlight. Spreading hydrated lime under the benches and around the greenhouse will also help to keep them under control.

Sowbugs. These are those many-legged oval-shaped insects about ½ inch long that you find under seed flats and flower pots, especially where it is damp. They roll into a ball when you expose them. Control is easy with a light 10 per cent DDT dust.

Rats, Mice and Moles. These rodents are easier to keep out of the greenhouse than to kill after they find their way in. They are particularly fond of tulip bulbs, lilies, and iris. In a greenhouse built with a concrete foundation, there is no problem. Otherwise, extend ½-inch-mesh galvanized wire about 2 feet below grade all around the greenhouse or lay it over the complete floor. Warfarin or Antu are good rodent killers. Fumigation will clean out nests and send the adults away temporarily, but they will return.

Diseases

Fungi and bacteria are the cause of most diseases. Many breed only under certain conditions of heat and moisture and are not especially troublesome in the small greenhouse where a reasonable amount of attention is paid to sanitation and the control of ventilation, temperature, humidity, and watering. Other diseases are caused by viruses. The following diseases are representative of those to watch out for in the greenhouse and methods for their control.

Leaf Spots are usually fungus or bacterial diseases, and may affect many plants such as asters, azaleas, begonias, roses, carnations, chrysanthemums, cyclamen, ivies, and pansies. The spots are a brownish black to rust color on the foliage, which may gradually become brown and droop.

The majority of leaf-spot organisms spread only in splashed water so they should be no problem in the greenhouse. Avoid splashing the foliage and stems at all times. If you do use overhead watering, by all means water in the morning when the drops will dry rapidly. Be sure to pick off and destroy infected foliage. If your all-purpose insecticide contains zineb it will give additional protection against both water-borne and air-borne disease organisms.

Mildew is a fungus disease with which everyone is familiar. It appears as a whitish coating on the leaves and stems of calendulas, chrysanthemums, hydrangeas, roses, and many others plants. Mildew is most troublesome in the fall and during rainy or moist seasons.

It can be prevented by maintaining an even temperature and avoiding drafts, sudden changes in temperature, and moisture on the foliage.

It is easily checked by dusting with fine sulfur. Better yet, when mildew is already established, is Mildex or Karathane at the rate of one-half to two-thirds teaspoon mixed in a gallon of water with a level teaspoon of Dreft as a spreader so the mildew growth will be thoroughly wet. Apply the spray when the greenhouse temperature is below 85° and when the spray will dry rapidly.

Botrytis Blight. This is those small, brown, rotted spots you see on flower petals and sometimes on foliage and stems. Bad cases appear as raised, gray, moldy fuzz. A cold, damp atmosphere and poor ventilation will cause it.

Pick off infected leaves and flowers and segregate plants. Dust or spray with zineb.

Damp-Off. This is a fungus disease that develops near the surface of the soil. You've probably noticed it when stems rot off at the base just as your seedlings seem to be doing the best. It also occurs on softwood cuttings and tender bulbous plants such as anemone or ranunculus.

Soil sterilization described in Chapter 6 is the best preventive measure, but if this isn't convenient, drench the soil with one of the new fungicides. Captan (Orthocide or Captan Fungicide) and Wilson's Anti-Damp are recent developments that give good control. Once started checking of damp-off and cutting-rot may be obtained by drenching the diseased spot and a border around it with Semesan, one scant teaspoon in a quart of water.

Stem Rot, Root Rot and Wilt are sometimes troublesome with a number of plants such as asters, calendula, chrysanthemums, cinerarias, calceolarias, carnations, delphinium, primulas and sweet peas. Poor drainage is often the cause of the trouble. The diseases will travel through the soil and attack healthy plants.

For control, discard infected plants. Use sterilized soil in clean benches and pots. Treat seeds and avoid watering from overhead. Use wilt-resistant seed. Propagate only from healthy plants.

Rust is a fungous disease which may affect asters, snapdragons, carnations, and chrysanthemums. It appears as rusty pustules on the stems and foliage, causing disfigurement or even death of the affected parts.

Destroy plants that are badly infected. Zineb and sulfur in the all-purpose spray above is particularly effective for rust control.

Virus Diseases. The virus is so small that it cannot even be detected with a microscope. It is in the sap of the plant. Sucking insects will carry it from infected to healthy plants. It is also carried in bulbs and cuttings. Stunt on chrysanthemums has become a serious virus disease, but mosaic diseases are probably more common. Sweet peas, petunias, roses, lilies, bulbous iris, gladiolus, daffodils, tulips, and dahlias are subject to mosaic viruses. Plants appear stunted and deformed, or are frequently streaked or mottled with yellow.

For control, destroy infected plants. Keep sucking insects under control. Buy bulbs and corms from reliable sources.

Sprayers and Dusters

A good brass or copper hand-sprayer will do a satisfactory job in the small greenhouse. Do not buy a cheap one. The best are not expensive. If the sprayer is good, it will build up a lasting pressure after a few strokes of the plunger and throw a finely divided mist that will completely cover the foliage. Such a sprayer will also serve to syringe the plants with water. The popular slide-type or trombone-type sprayers which suck the spray from a pail or other container should prove extremely satisfactory for the small greenhouse.

In larger greenhouses or orchid houses, an electric motor-driven sprayer is a good investment. Select one that has the capacity to develop at least 150 pounds of pressure. Never allow an insecticide or fungicide to remain in the sprayer. Rinse it out with clear water each time after using.

A hand duster that has a nozzle which can be adjusted to throw the dust up underneath the foliage is best both for the greenhouse and garden. In small greenhouses, a large rubber spray-bulb can be used. Remove the nozzle, fill the bulb partly full with dust, and replace the nozzle.

Seed Treatment

Seeds sometimes decay due to fungi and bacteria that are carried on the seed or are present in the soil. It is a simple matter to treat them with a disinfectant against this danger. Tests have proven that better quality is obtained with most varieties when treated.

Several excellent disinfectants are available but are not well suited to all. Arasan is one of the best and safest for general purposes. Semesan and Captan are also good.

Helpful Practices

The important thing is to recognize the presence of insects and diseases and carry out a periodic schedule of spraying or fumigating. On the other hand, do not spray just for the sake of spraying or more often than is necessary for good control. Just as you watch the quality of the growth your plants make from day to day, watching out for insects and diseases and taking the precautionary measures necessary, soon becomes a natural practice. A magnifying glass proves helpful in detecting some of the small insects.

The following suggestions will prove helpful in prevention and control of insects and diseases: Buy seeds, bulbs, corms and rhizomes from reliable dealers and treat with a disinfectant before planting. Use wilt- and rust-resistant seeds of asters and snapdragons. Make cuttings from disease-free stock plants and root in clean sand.

Use sterilized soil and change after each major crop, or at the end of each season. See Chapter 6.

Form sanitary habits. Do not throw dead foliage in walks or under benches. Keep the greenhouse clean and free from dirty pots, flats, and rubbish. Keep tools and benches clean. A formaldehyde solution, 1 part 40 per cent formaldehyde with 50 parts water, makes a good disinfectant for washing pots, tools, benches and for spraying on walks and underneath benches. Paint the inside of the greenhouse every five years.

Pick off and destroy diseased foliage and blooms. Discard badly infected plants. If they are too valuable to part with, isolate them from other plants.

Always handle plants carefully. Do not injure them in transplanting or shifting and so leave them vulnerable to disease.

Do not crowd plants together. Set them far enough apart to permit free circulation of air between plants.

Inspect all plants carefully before bringing them into the greenhouse. Spray, dust, or fumigate, if necessary, to prevent infestation of other plants.

Water with care. Avoid overwatering and wetting foliage or water splashing on plants. Water in the morning, and on bright days when possible, when the temperature is rising, to allow for evaporation before nightfall. Condensation on foliage when the temperature is dropping is sure to cause trouble.

Maintain a clean, fresh atmosphere by careful control

of the ventilation, temperature, and moisture. Fungus diseases run riot under conditions of excessive moisture; red spider and nematodes under conditions of dryness.

Do not permit aphids, mites and other insects to breed. In addition to the damage they themselves cause, they spread disease. Spray, dust, and fumigate periodically as a precautionary measure. Don't wait until plants become infested.

At first some of the precautionary measures suggested may seem unnecessary. In fact, many professional growers are able to produce good crops without resorting to most of them, while others claim they make the difference between profit and loss. In any event, the effort required is so trivial, and the degree of safety promised so great, that this seems worth while.

Take a treatment of seeds, for instance. Some authorities question its value. Yet it takes just a minute or two to do, and the cost is negligible, so why not play safe? Similarly, soil sterilization is simple with modern preparations. Measuring out a little formaldehyde to put in the water used for washing tools, benches, and pots and keeping a covered can on hand in which to throw diseased foliage and rubbish are easy precautions in the small greenhouse. After a short time, such things become mechanical, and you do them as a matter of routine.

Insecticides are being improved all the time so any recommendations given this month may be outdated next month. But the material we have today can well be credited with increasing our yield from greenhouse plants as much as 50 to 60 per cent, thanks to the splendid research efforts of our pathologists and entomologists at agricultural schools, colleges, and industrial firms.

The following dilution table may prove helpful in mixing insecticides and fungicides that come in liquid form:

Dilutions	Tablespoons for 1 Gallon Water
1 to 1000	¼
1 to 750	⅓
1 to 500	½
1 to 250	1
1 to 200	1¼
1 to 150	1⅔
1 to 100 (approximately 1%)	2½
1 to 50 (approximately 2%)	5
1 to 33 (approximately 3%)	7½
1 to 25 (approximately 4%)	10
1 to 20 (approximately 5%)	12½ (about ¾ cup)
1 to 10 (approximately 10%)	25 (about 1½ cups)

20

Automatic Watering and Soil-less Culture

This chapter is not for real green-thumb gardeners who are fortunate enough to have the time, feel, and know-how to get good results by the usual methods. It is for those less fortunate, busy people whose work or other obligations prevents them from spending all the time they would like in gardening—people who want to have flowers in abundance but who must garden when odd moments are available and when they have the inclination. It is also for those less skilled who would appreciate the mechanical help that takes the guesswork out of gardening.

With these gardeners in mind, horticultural investigators and engineers spent many years in the development of equipment and methods for automatic growing. Some of the results are the soil tensiometer, automatic watering, soil-less culture, automatic ventilation, and heating equipment.

Automatic Watering

It should be understood at the outset that as with all so-called "automatic gadgets," automatic watering is actually only semiautomatic. It does permit you to leave the greenhouse for long periods of time, and it must be adjusted to the particular season and crop and individual set of conditions.

How much water should we give our plants, and when? How much in a clay soil, a sandy soil, or a soil high in organic matter? Isn't it true that you have been impressed with the uncertainty of just how much to water ever since you started gardening?

Automatic watering, as developed at Cornell University by Prof. Kenneth Post, has solved this problem for us and has numerous other advantages as well.

Most of us have seen the soil in our seed flats, in small pots, and sometimes even in large pots, become packed and crusty after just a short time without proper watering. We know, too, how much better and more evenly moist the soil becomes when the pots and flats are set in a tray of water so they can draw up their own moisture from the bottom through the drainage holes. Automatic watering does just this kind of watering job under mechanical control. You don't have to worry about whether your plants are getting sufficient water if there is no one about to look after them while you are away.

What's more, automatic watering does a better job than is possible by surface watering. The soil is kept more evenly wet from top to bottom, and root growth is far better than when the soil is allowed to become dry between watering periods. The soil does not become compressed and packed down but continues to remain loose and to contain oxygen so necessary to healthy plant growth. There is less danger of fungous diseases. The subirrigation method of automatic watering eliminates splashing of water which spreads the spores. And that morning rush many of us experience several times a week is eliminated—the rush necessary when we are late and which results in hurriedly sloshing water on the plants before dashing off for the office.

Soil Tensiometer

An instrument that measures the tension with which moisture is held in the soil is called a soil tensiometer. It is a valuable guide that tells you when to water, and how much to water, or when not to water—if the soil is too wet.

It has a porous cup that is placed in the soil and a vacuum gauge that registers the moisture tension. The tensiometer is filled with water which moves in and out of the porous cup and equalizes with the tension both inside and outside the cup. The reading on the vacuum gauge records the tension with which the water is held by the soil particles. A soil tensiometer is practically essential when automatic watering of bench crops is used, for it lets you know the condition of the soil moisture at all times.

Soils

The same types of soil you now use in pots or benches are suitable with automatic watering. This method of watering is particularly desirable for the greenhouse gardener who is forced to get along with soils that tend to pack down under surface watering, forming a hard top crust. In fact, poor sandy loam is safer than soils too high in organic matter. It is not necessary to mulch, but it is usually desirable to add peat moss to condition clay soils. Soils that are loose and tend to lose capillarity, (that is soils that are made up of large particles), may have to be surface watered about once a month. Fertilizer may be applied in liquid or dry form. In applying dry fertilizer, wash it in by surface watering.

Automatic Watering of Bench Crops

Equipment consists of a watertight bench for watering by subirrigation. Three-eighth-inch copper tubing provides good connection from your water supply to the bench. Your local plumbing supply house has the tubing

A water-tight bench is easily arranged for automatic watering or gravel culture.

and the flanged fittings necessary for fastening it to the bottom of the bench.

The bench must be absolutely watertight. A wooden bench can be waterproofed by spreading Vinyl plastic cloth over the bottom and sides. For a more permanent waterproofing job use a phenol resin product called Kendex, made by the Kendall Oil Company of Bradford, Pennsylvania. It melts at low temperatures and stays soft to fill cracks up to ⅛ inch wide and make them watertight.

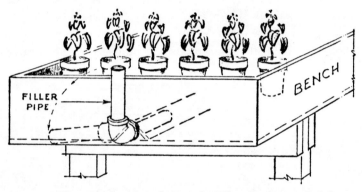

Automatic Watering by Manual Control. Filler pipe is attached finger-tight at elbow so it can be raised or lowered to control the water level for subirrigation from the bottom of the bench. Water is injected into pipe with a hose; pipe is lowered sideways to drain off surplus.

It is important to make sure the benches are strong enough in the first place to carry the load. Steel, aluminum, or asbestos board may be used. Metal benches should be coated with agricultural asphalt to eliminate anything toxic to plant growth.

A conductor is used to carry the water from one end of the bench to the other. This can be a half-round tile, a steel angle, or an *inverted* V made by nailing two boards together.

Pea gravel is placed an inch deep in the bottom of the bench, and the soil is placed on top. Both the gravel and soil must be level. This insures even distribution of moisture. Water makes the best guide for leveling the gravel and soil. Flood the bench to the desired height of the gravel smoothing it out with a board.

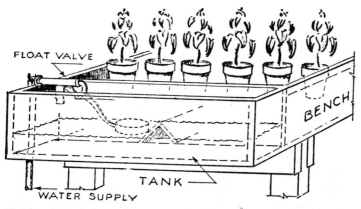

This bench is set up with pea gravel and sand so plants can draw up moisture by capillary attraction. Notice installation of the small poultry waterer float valve that maintains a constant level of water for the plants.

The water may be fed manually through a tile or flower pot extending down through the gravel to the bottom of the bench or through an elbow and nipple connected to the end of the bench. This filler pipe is attached finger-tight at the elbow so it can be raised or lowered to control the height of the water for subirrigation. After the water has remained in the bottom long enough to draw up what is needed by capillary attraction, the surplus is drained off.

Water may also be fed automatically by a constant water-level method. A small float-valve of the type used to water poultry is installed in one end of the bench, as illustrated. The level is maintained about ½ inch below the soil. By keeping it this low, there is little danger of getting it too wet, and your soil tensiometer will tell you whether the level is high enough to supply the moisture needed. The float-valve can also be set in a galvanized steel box alongside the bench, if it is more convenient.

As with many so-called automatic things, the system of watering requires checking from time to time. It is very easy to get the soil too wet in winter—especially if it contains a great deal of manure. I have always found it safer to use the injection method in winter, except during periods when I'm away for a week or two. At such times the constant water-level method is better.

In my first greenhouse book, I went into much detail about a complete system of automatic watering using an electric soil-tensiometer, time switch, and solenoid valve, but the equipment was so involved that many amateurs who tried it had difficulty. I am, therefore, omitting it from this book, but those who seek this detailed information can get it from bulletins issued by their State Agricultural College or experiment stations.

Potted Plants

Automatic watering makes its biggest saving in time and labor when applied to potted plants. You will find it particularly advantageous for small plants in 2- and 3-inch pots that sometimes require watering as much as two or three times a day. When they are watered by this automatic system, you will hardly have to bother with them until they are ready to shift into larger pots.

You will be particularly pleased to find that this method of watering will keep the soil moisture even, and the roots will be more uniformly distributed throughout the entire ball than when potted plants are surface watered. Undoubtedly, this is because surface watering tends to concentrate moisture toward the outside and bottom of the ball.

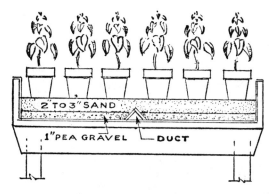

The illustration shows a setup with the watertight plant bench filled with 1 inch of pea gravel covered by a layer of 2 to 3 inches of coarse sand. Pots are best placed with small and large sizes grouped separately, for the surface soil in each pot should be 6 inches above the water surface. This is easily accomplished by using a deep layer of sand under small pots and a shallow layer under large pots.

In potting the plants, no drainage crock is placed in the bottom, for the soil within the pots must come in direct contact with the moist sand from which water is drawn up by capillary attraction. In order to start capillarity, it is necessary first to water the surface of the pot and again whenever it is allowed to become dry. Nourishment is best applied with liquid fertilizer.

Surface Sprinkler Method

A variation of automatic watering, that does not require watertight benches, makes use of plastic or rubber tubing with pinpoint openings or small distributing nozzles spaced to permit a trickle of water into the soil. The water moves to the edge of the bench and to the spaces between the pinpoint openings by capillary movement. The soil does not pack down nor is it disturbed in any way by the application of water. One of these systems even takes care of plants in large pots or tubs. Nutrients are lost more rapidly than by the other systems, but provisions can be made for automatic feeding with watering.

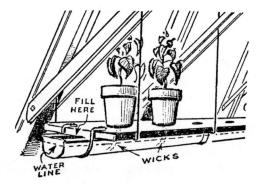

Plants on Shelves

Automatic watering also works out particularly well when used for potted plants and seed flats on shelves. It eliminates the painstaking care required when hand watering to avoid the dripping and splashing of water on the foliage of plants in the bench below. It also eliminates the frequent watering needed by plants close to the glass that dry out more rapidly.

Automatic watering is very simple with glass wicks. One end of the wick is frayed and flattened out on the bottom of the pot or flat, as pictured. The other end is placed in a reservoir. Individual saucers are sometimes

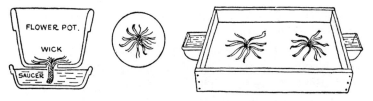

Self-watering pots and flats with glass wicks.

used for each plant, but for automatic watering on a larger and more practical scale, a galvanized steel gutter is attached to the underside of the shelf. Holes or slots are cut in the shelf through which the wick can pass into the gutter reservoir. A 4-inch gutter will probably hold sufficient water to last a week or more. Using a hose to keep it filled is a simple matter.

Seed flats used for automatic watering must be watertight, but this is easy with asphalt paper or Vinyl plastic cloth.

Soil-less Culture

Soil-less culture is widely used outdoors in areas where good soil is not available or where growing conditions are not healthful. Our government made large installations in the Pacific Islands and Japan during the war. They are still in use today producing food for the men in our armed forces.

Small installations are practical in the greenhouse. I had excellent results over a five-year period with a system that originated at Ohio State University.

In addition to its great convenience, soil-less culture is a highly productive method for the amateur to follow. Superior yields to those produced in good greenhouse soils are not claimed for it, but through its use gardeners located where access to good soil is difficult can achieve results that more nearly approach quality. More accurate control of the nutrients on which the plants feed is possible than with the average soil found in greenhouses. Deficiencies and excesses of nutrients are controllable. Toxicities can be eliminated. Soil diseases, insects, and weed seeds are not present, so the big job of soil sterilization necessary to good soil is not required.

Anyone who can follow directions can prepare the solutions and operate the equipment, which has done much to mechanize growing. Crops are uniform, and successes can be duplicated again and again by following previous procedures. Of course the environment necessary to healthy plant growth is the same as with crops in soil. Proper conditions of light, fresh air, humidity and temperature must be maintained.

Gravel Culture. Of the various methods of soil-less culture, gravel culture is the most popular. The sketches and photographs show the equipment. It consists of a simple, watertight V-bottom bench with a tank or reservoir underneath to hold the nutrient solution. The bench and reservoir may be of wood or steel, painted on the inside with an asphalt emulsion that is not toxic to plant life.

The plants are set in clean gravel, and get their food

and nourishment from a nutrient solution. This is done by flooding the gravel periodically by subirrigation. A small electric pump conducts the solution from the reservoir, through a rubber hose to the bottom of the plant bench. An electric time-switch, which can be set to turn the current on and off as many as three or four times a day, automatically starts and stops the pump at predetermined intervals. The solution is siphoned back into the reservoir through an overflow when it reaches the desired height.

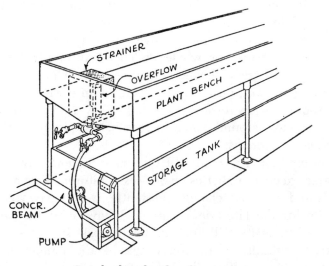

Gravel culture bench and equipment.

The gravel or other medium used to support the plants in the benches should be of material that will not break down or give off elements which would have a detrimental effect on the solution, such as large proportions of limestone (which would raise the alkalinity or precipitate the phosphate). A small proportion of limestone is desirable, however, say 10 to 15 per cent. Silica gravel, granite chips, trap rock are satisfactory. Cinders may be used, but must be thoroughly leached and free from sulfur. One-fourth to ⅜ inch is a good size for the medium.

Many solutions for soil-less culture have been developed at agricultural experiment stations and agricultural colleges. All serve the same purpose of providing the elements essential to plant growth in a form that is available. There is no one formula that is the best for every crop, but there are several good general-purpose formulas to choose from. Availability of the ingredients may be the chief factor in influencing the selection.

The salts are very inexpensive, and may be purchased at any drugstore or wholesale chemical supply house. Commercial grade chemicals may be used. The salts may be weighed out, mixed dry, and stored in cardboard cartons or glass jars for use as needed. They are not dangerous to have around, since in reasonable quantities they are not poisonous.

Many State Agricultural Experiment Stations have prepared excellent bulletins on Soil-less Culture. Since methods and formulas change constantly, it will pay you to write for the latest information. I have used the Ohio State University WP Formula for the past six years with excellent results. In the following table the numbers indicate ounces per 100 gallons of water.

CHEMICALS	OHIO STATE FORMULA WP
Potassium nitrate	9.4
Ammonium sulfate	1.5
Magnesium sulfate (Epsom Salts)	7.3
Monocalcium phosphate	3.8
Calcium sulfate	8.0

Manganous sulfate should be added to the solutions. One ounce of manganous sulfate is dissolved in one gallon of water acidified with three or five drops of commercial sulfuric acid. About a tenth of this solution should be used for 100 gallons of nutrient solution. Iron should be added in the form of ferrous sulfate at the rate of four ounces per 100 gallons. Add the same amount each week.

A single-strength WP solution should be used for the first month on all newly planted crops. When the plants have become well established, usually after three to six weeks, the concentration should be doubled. Twice the amount of chemicals per 100 gallons of water recommended in the WP solution should be used.

In the small greenhouse the test for deficiencies need not worry the amateur. If the solution is changed once a month, a test for acidity about every ten days should be all that is needed. If the solution is used for longer periods deficiency tests are necessary, but in the small greenhouse the quantity of solution is not so great or so expensive as to make a change of solution each month an expensive or troublesome job.

It is surprising how plants will grow in gravel culture on almost pure water, and I believe that, with all other conditions for growing favorable, the quality of growth in soil-less culture is directly comparable with that of soil. If the nutrient solution is correctly maintained, results will be of high quality. If not, they will be lower, in a degree comparable to growing in mediocre or poor soils.

The pH scale is used for the acidity test. Seven is the neutral point, and all numbers below 7 indicate acidity; all above, alkalinity. The elements are available to most plants with a slightly acid solution, one that ranges from pH 6.5 to 7. Some plants, such as gardenias, like a more acid solution—pH 5.5. In a few cases, a slightly akaline solution is wanted—pH 7 to 7.5, but above that most plants will suffer.

Stock solutions for lowering or raising the pH can be made by dissolving one ounce of concentrated sulfuric acid in a gallon of water to lower the acidity, or two ounces of sodium hydroxide in a gallon of water to raise it.

To test for acidity, the simple nitrozene papers are satisfactory. Your druggist has them, and you will find they are very inexpensive. An accurate acidity test and complete test for deficiencies and excesses of nutrients, however, calls for a good soil-testing kit.

Plants can be set in the gravel with a small ball of soil around them. The roots soon spread out into the gravel. Some growers wash the soil off the roots to keep the gravel clean, but this causes some check in growth. The drainage of the bench must be good or the roots may rot.

The number of times the switch is set to pump the solution depends upon the season of the year, the size of the plants, and the kind of gravel used. In summer, three to four pumpings daily may be required; in winter, one or two. The quality of the growth you want will determine the number of pumpings. Pumping is always done in the daytime. The solution is allowed to come up to about one inch from the surface of the gravel. This prevents the growth of algae. An adjustable overflow controls the height the solution reaches in the bench.

Garden Frames

Y our GLASS GARDEN need not be large or expensive for you to enjoy the fine results that are possible. In a hot bed or heated pit frame, you can grow anything that can be grown in a greenhouse. The difference is that a greenhouse is more comfortable to work in and easier to manage. It requires less attention because the factors needed for healthy plant culture are under simpler control. If you grow flowers with whole-hearted enthusiasm in your home and garden you will have double the success under glass, and should, at least, have some cold-frames or hot beds. The many ways in which they will serve you will greatly repay you for your time and expense.

Garden frames have many functions other than the usual raising of plants early in spring for the summer garden. They also have many valuable uses throughout the year. In summer they may be used for raising plants of perennials or biennials, and for growing plants from cuttings of ornamental and flowering shrubs, trees, peren-

217

nials, vines and house plants. In fall they may be used for sowing seeds of annuals that will germinate earlier and better in spring. In winter they give needed protection to young plants of perennials, biennials and semi-hardy perennials. In spring and fall they may be used for raising crops of spinach, lettuce and radishes; in fall they give protection to parsley, chives, Swiss chard and other greens, so that you can have them long after outdoor plants are gone. A coldframe is almost a necessary adjunct to a greenhouse throughout the year. It is used for hardening-off young plants to prepare them for setting out in the garden in spring. For curing bulbs and flowering shrubs for winter blooming, and for storing stock plants of chrysanthemums during winter; and most of all for raising the young plants during summer and fall that are to be the flowers of the winter garden.

Early Plants from Seeds

You can't beat a frame for raising plants of many kinds. They grow better in the humid atmosphere of the small enclosure than they do in a greenhouse. Perhaps it is because they are close to the glass. Try seeds of calendula, annual dahlias, pansies, cabbage, broccoli and lettuce. Seedling plants for the summer garden can be started during April in the coldframe and the end of February in the hot bed. Before planting, the sash should be set in place for several days on the coldframe, and the heat controlled in the hot bed to make sure the temperature is right. Seeds are planted directly in soil placed in the frame, or in flats or bulb pots. The use of flats or pots is good because the seeds may be sown earlier, and kept in the house until the frames are warm enough to take them.

TIME FOR PLANTING VEGETABLES UNDER GLASS

CROP	*SOW SEED IN COLDFRAME	SOW SEED IN HOT BED OR GREENHOUSE	AVERAGE NUMBER OF DAYS TO MATURITY	SAFE TIME FOR SETTING OUT PLANTS	TIME OF HARVEST	SEEDS FOR 100 FT. ROW	INCHES BETWEEN ROWS	DISTANCE BETWEEN PLANTS IN ROW (IN.)	AVERAGE YIELD OF 100 FT. ROW
Cabbage Early†	April 1st	Feb. 25th	90	April 1st	July 1st	1 pkt.	30	18	45-55 heads
Cabbage Late†	May 15th	March 1st	100	July 1st	Oct. 1st	1 pkt.	30	18	45-55 heads
Broccoli†	April 1st	March 1st	90	April 15th	July 1st	1 pkt.	30	24	45 bu. flowers
Cauliflower†	April 15th	March 1st	100-130	April 15th	July 20th	1 pkt.	30	20	40-50 heads
Cantaloupe	April 15th	April 20th	90-110	May 15th	Aug. 10th	½ oz.	60	48‡	6-8 fruit per hill
Celery†	April 15th	Feb. 15th	120-150	May 1st	Aug. 1st	1 pkt.	24	5	200 bunches
Corn Early†	April 15th	April 1st	65-100	May 10th	July 1st	4 oz.	30	24	4 dozen
Cucumber	April 15th	March 20th	60-80	May 20th	June 20th	½ oz.	60	48	200
Lettuce Leaf	April 1st	March 1st	30-45	April 10th	May 15th	¼ oz.	12	8	Cut until July 15
Lettuce Head	April 1st	March 1st	60-100	April 10th	June 1st	¼ oz.	12	12	70 heads
Endive	April 1st	March 1st	60-90	April 15th	May 15th	1 pkt.	18	15	65 plants
Onions†	April 1st	March 1st	110-130	May 1st	June 15th	¼ oz.	14	3	1½-2 bu.
Peppers†	April 15th	March 15th	125-150	May 15th	Aug. 15th to frost	1 pkt.	30	20	5 bu.
Beets	April 1st	March 15th	45-60	April 10th	June 15th	1 oz.	15	3	2½ bu.
Spinach	April 1st	March 15th	45	April 1st	May 1st	½ oz.	12	4	3 bu.
Tomatoes†	April 15th	March 15th	100-140	May 15th	July 10th	½ oz.	48	48	4 bu.
Brussel Sprouts	April 1st	March 15th	130-150	May 25th	July on	1 pkt.	30	18	30 qts.
Parsley†	April 1st	Feb. 1st	65-80	April 1st	July 1st	1 pkt.	16	4	90 bunches
Watermelon†	April 15th	March 1st	110-140	May 15th	Aug. to frost	1 oz.	72	72	40
Egg Plant†	April 15th	March 1st	140-160	May 15th	Aug. 1st to frost	1 pkt.	48	48	125
Beans Snap	April 15th	April 10th	45-60	May 10th	June 10th	1 lb.	30	3	2 bu.
Swiss Chard	April 1st	March 1st	60-75	May 15th	June 15th to frost	1 oz.	18	6	Cut until frost

Based on conditions 100 miles North and South of New York, N. Y.
* Assuming coldframe will be covered at night.

‡ Distance between hills in a row.
† Usually grown from transplanted plants only.

Ventilation is perhaps the most important job in taking care of the garden frame. Too much ventilation during cold weather will chill the plants; too little during warm weather may "cook" them. It doesn't take long for the sun's heat to warm up the small area of the frame. In cold weather, the sash opened just a crack will answer, but never open it when the temperature is below freezing, even to take a look inside, for tender plants are easily nipped. In warm weather, the sash can be elevated on a long, notched stick.

During cold nights, burlap bags filled with leaves or mats of straw are placed over the beds to protect them and conserve heat. During warm, sunny days, slats are placed over the frames to shade delicate young plants from the burning rays of the sun.

Planting Time
For Sowing Tender and Half Hardy Annuals

Of course, the same things that apply to the vegetable garden apply also to the flowers in your garden. How often have you sighed because the season wasn't long enough and your annuals were frostbitten just as they promised to bloom? By starting them early under glass, you will have blooms three to four weeks earlier. Here is a chart giving the planting time in a greenhouse, hot bed or coldframe. The plants can be set out in the garden as soon as all danger of frost is over.

Hardening-Off

Plants that are raised in the greenhouse or home are naturally tender because of the higher temperature and

	GREENHOUSE	HOT BED	COLDFRAME
Vinca rosea	January	March	April 1
Begonia semperflorens	January	March	April 1
Verbena rigida (venosa)	January	March	April 1

Tropical Bedding Plants

Grevillea robusta	January	March	April 1
Musa Ensete	January	March	April 1
Snapdragons (in variety)	February	March	April 1
Verbena hortensis	February	March	April 1
Carnations (border types)	February	March	April 1
Dianthus chinensis	February	March	April 1
Heddewigii		March	April 1
Hibiscus manihot	February		
Hunnemannia fumari- aefolia (in pots)	February	March	April 1
Lobelia	March (1st 2 wks.)	March 15	April 1
Nierembergia	March (1st 2 wks.)	March 15	April 1
Salpiglossis	March (1st 2 wks.)	March 15	April 1
Browallia	March (1st 2 wks.)	March 15	April 1
Petunia	March (1st 2 wks.)	March 15	April 1
Arctotis	March (1st 2 wks.)	March 15	April 1
Gomphrena	March (1st 2 wks.)	March 15	April 1
Ageratum	March (1st 2 wks.)	March 15	April 1
Gilia	March (1st 2 wks.)	March 15	April 1

Gray Foliage Annuals

Bachelor Buttons (Centaurea candidissima) (Centaurea gymnocarpa)	March (1st 2 wks.)	March 15	April 1
Cineraria maritima Diamond	March (1st 2 wks.)	March 15	April 1
Artemisia sacrorum viridis	March (1st 2 wks.)	March 15	April 1
All varieties of Mari- gold (Tagetes)	March (last 2 wks.)	March 15	April 1
China Aster	March (last 2 wks.)	March 15	April 1
Cosmos	March (last 2 wks.)	March 15	April 1
Zinnias	March (last 2 wks.)	March 15	April 1
Salvia	March (last 2 wks.)	March 15	April 1
Nicotiana	March (last 2 wks.)	March 15	April 1
Stocks	March (last 2 wks.)	March 15	April 1
Calendula	March (last 2 wks.)	March 15	April 1

(Most half-hardy annuals can be sown at this time, assuming coldframe will be covered at night.)

	GREENHOUSE	HOT BED	COLDFRAME
*Annual Vines—*Preferably in Pots			
Morning Glory	April	April 1	April 15
Cobæa scandens	April	April 1	April 15
Balloon vine (Cardiospermum)	April	April 1	April 15
Balsam Apple (Momordica)	April	April 1	April 15
Cardinal Climber (Quamoclit)	April	April 1	April 15
Climbing Bean (Dolichos)	April	April 1	April 15
Allegheny Vine (Adlumia)	April	April 1	April 15
Castor Oil Plant (Ricinus)	April	April 1	April 15
Summer Cypress (Kochia)	April	April 1	April 15

protected conditions under which they were raised. To set them out in the garden during the early springtime, when days seem warm enough but nights are still cold and frosty, would check their growth. Plants cannot adapt themselves to sudden changes, and once checked this way they never again have full ability to draw up moisture and take in nourishment. They seldom die, but seem to stand still and finally turn out to be pathetic-looking, little, stunted plants.

In the coldframe, seedlings can be adjusted gradually to meet the new climatic conditions. When they are first put into the frames, the sash is opened a crack for a short period during the day. Gradually the opening is increased, and the ventilation period is lengthened until it extends from early in the day on into the night. After ten or twelve days, the sash is left off entirely.

Plants from Seed in Summer

The garden frame is the place to grow plants from seeds that should be sown in late spring and summer for flowering the following year: perennials, biennials, and half-hardy perennials such as dianthus, bellis, campanula, and pansies. The enclosure acts as a shield from the hot air currents that dry out the surface of the soil and increase the transpiration rate of plants when they are out in the open. It is easily shaded to reduce evaporation and hold in the moisture that is so essential to germination and the growth of tender plants.

Rooting Cuttings

By the same principles, the coldframe or hot bed makes an excellent spot for a propagating bed to root cuttings of ornamental and flowering shrubs, as covered in Chapter 17. The coldframe can be used from late spring to early fall, and the hot bed over a longer season. The gentle bottom heat of the hot bed promotes rooting. The glazed sash helps keep the temperature and humidity of the air surrounding the cuttings where it should be, and under close control.

Winter Protection

Young perennials, biennials and semihardy plants that need good protection during winter can be put in no safer place than the coldframe. Chrysanthemums, myosotis, gaillardia, violas, pansies, primula, pyrethrum, and the like, covered with dry leaves or salt hay and left in the frame all winter with the sash mats and shutters in place will get the conditions of air and moisture they need to carry them through the severest of winters. Burlap bags filled with dried leaves serve as good mats. During winter the plants will require no attention whatsoever, but in spring as growth starts they will need a gradual hardening-off period just as with tender seedlings, as described above.

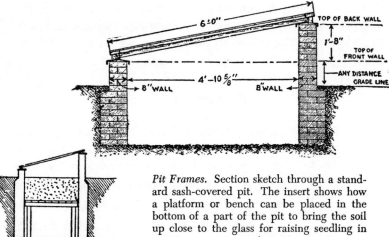

Pit Frames. Section sketch through a standard sash-covered pit. The insert shows how a platform or bench can be placed in the bottom of a part of the pit to bring the soil up close to the glass for raising seedling in spring.

Bulb Blooms

Tulips, hyacinths, daffodils, and iris can be had in flower in the home or greenhouse during the winter if the bulbs are potted in fall and stored in the frame until well rooted. They are brought indoors two to four weeks after the root systems are well developed. (See Chapter 10.) They may also be planted right in the frame and forced into bloom several weeks earlier than the outdoor ones.

The Frame-Covered Pit

The frame-covered pit should be 2 or more feet deep. It is frequently used for winter storage of flowering shrubs such as azaleas, hydrangeas, potted roses, and hardy plants of delphinium and campanula that are rested in a cold house until they are wanted for forcing into bloom in the greenhouse during winter. When heated, you can grow in it just as you do in the greenhouse—snapdragons, cornflowers, fuchsias, geraniums, primroses, stock, candytuft, feverfew and practically anything you choose. Without any heat at all, or just a moderate amount, it can be used to carry plants of many varieties through the winter, if the building is well constructed and the glass insulated with mats and shutters. Of course, the plants will not make much growth or produce much in the way of flowers from December until the end of March, but as the sunlight becomes stronger in spring, the plants will quickly respond and reward you with a wealth of bloom.

Some enthusiasts choose to build a deep pit-frame house and install heat and plant benches, rather than a greenhouse, because it seems so simple to construct with its solid walls and sash roof. This appeals to the imagination because almost anyone can figure how they can easily build one at the cost of next to nothing, but such houses are not so easy to build well and are often damp as a cellar. In comparison with a small prefabricated greenhouse the deep pit-frame house is not a bargain except when used as a large coldframe or storage house. The greenhouse on a raised foundation with glass sides and roof provides much more of that most important of factors that really counts—LIGHT. You realize how much during the dead of winter when light is at a premium and your plants seem to stand still.

Garden Frame Construction

Hot beds and coldframes are easy and inexpensive to build. You can make them from window sash that you may have on hand or can procure readily in your neighborhood, or you can buy the sash in several sizes from a greenhouse manufacturer or sash mill. If you buy sash, select those made of cypress. Cypress lasts longer than other woods when exposed to extreme conditions of moisture.

The first step in building the frame is to select a good site. It should be protected from the cold, prevailing northwest winter winds, and must be fully exposed to the east and south for best results. It should also be located where drainage is good. That is, in a spot where surface water from rains will not collect and settle.

Hot bed sash is made in three sizes—3 by 6 feet, the standard size; 3 by 3 feet, just half the standard size, and 2 by 4 feet, a convenient light-weight size. The sides of the garden frame can be purchased knocked-down and all ready to put together with nuts and bolts, but you can easily make them if you have the lumber available.

The first step is to build a frame of 2-inch boards, as illustrated. Heavier wood may be used if you happen to have it. The frame should be 16 inches high in the back, and 12 inches high in the front, to permit drainage of rain water from the surface of the sash.

When permanency is wanted, the sides of the frame are built of poured concrete, or concrete or cinder blocks. For poured concrete, a mixture of one part cement, two-

and-a-half parts of sand and five parts of gravel is adequate. If you have never worked with concrete before, you should try it. It is fun. The forms for pouring the concrete can be made of any boards you happen to have about. After the concrete is poured, the top edge of the frame is capped with a steel or wooden sill, as shown in the pictures. Of course, the masonry walls should extend below frost.

Between each sash, a rafter is placed to support the sash and carry off water that flows between the sashes. There are grooves in it to carry off water when it rains.

Some gardeners like to divide their garden frames into two sections, using one section as an electric hot bed, and the other as a coldframe. When used as a coldframe, it is wise to have a floor of cinders 6 to 8 inches deep. Cinders are easier to keep free from fungous diseases than soil and make an excellent material into which pots can be plunged for holding moisture. It is also a good idea to plant seeds in bulb pans and seed flats rather than directly in soil, because they can be cared for and handled much more easily when in containers. Furthermore, if a fungous disease should start in one section of the bed, the infected plants can be removed to prevent spreading.

Electric Hot Beds

If you plan to heat one section, or a whole bed, electricity really offers the easiest and most permanent means of doing this. It gives a steadier heat than the old-fashioned manure method, and is much cleaner to handle. Plastic or lead-covered electric cable is available for the purpose, and is furnished with a thermostat that regulates the temperature to whatever degree is wanted. The expense of using it is not prohibitive where electric rates are around 3 cents per kilowatt-hour, because the current is only on during the night and on dull days. On sunny days, practically no electricity is used. The plan shows how the cable should be installed for "bottom heat."

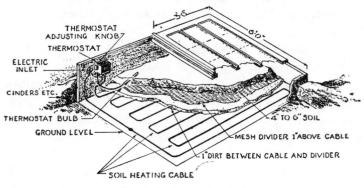

Electrically heated hot bed.

Another good way of installing the electric cable is to hang it upon hooks placed in the side of the garden frame. Less electricity is used this way but, of course, you do not get the advantage of "bottom heat" which is good for giving seedlings their first push.

Manure Heated Hot Beds

A manure heated bed is constructed the same as the one described for electricity, but it requires a pit about 3 feet deep underneath to hold the manure. Hot manure is put into this pit several weeks before the frame is to be used, and let stand until the fermentation begins to slow down. A thermometer is put into the bed to register the temperature. In the beginning, it will be well over 100°, but

within a week or so will drop to 90°. Then, about 4 inches
of good composted soil can be put in on top of the manure,
and the bed can be used. The manure will maintain heat
for about four or five weeks—just long enough to give you
the good head-start you want. When you are finished
with the hot bed, the manure can be used in your compost pile or garden.

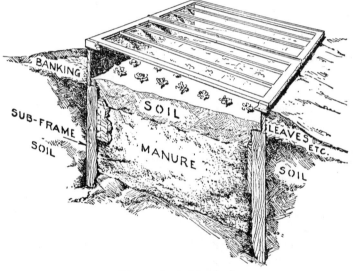

Manure heated hot bed.

Sash-Covered Pits

Sash-covered pits are usually built with a single sash
across masonry walls, or with double sash supported by a
ridge in the center. The excavation is made to a depth
required for the height of the plants to be stored or
grown. Walls extend below frost. Only the best sash
lumber should be used—clear, sap-free cypress or red-

wood. These are the lumbers which last when exposed to the weather—ordinary lumber will rot out in one to five years' time.

The south end of the double sash pit is usually of glazed construction with a door, the north end of solid concrete or wood. The pit should be built on high ground where there is good natural drainage. It will be utterly useless if built where water can seep in so that it gets damp and musty like a wet cellar.

22

How to Earn Extra Dollars

Your home greenhouse can be made to pay for itself and then some, if you sell your surplus flowers and plants. What an excellent hobby and also a means to extra income after retirement! It is like growing extra dollars right in your own back yard. With some people, it is a planned business investment right from the start, with others the enterprise just seems to happen. But perhaps I can best illustrate with actual cases.

Edna Roberts, a housewife in Maine, started with eighty-five African violets. Visiting neighbors continually asked, "Won't you sell me just one plant?" Practically every greenhouse gardener knows how that is, but Mrs. Roberts didn't even have a greenhouse. She sold plants and propagated more and more until they took up so much space, either plants or family had to go.

In most cases all this would have led to a greenhouse, but in this one, it led to an abandoned chicken coop. With boards, glass, paint, and an oil stove, the little build-

ing was revamped and decorated with a bright sign—
African Violets.

More and more neighbors beat a path to the door and
so vigorously that a large greenhouse was soon possible.
A greater variety of plants was grown; gloxinias, achimenes, and other African-violet relatives, fancy-leaved
geraniums, spring bedding-plants, and ever so many
others. Mrs. Roberts then exhibited in the flower shows
and won prize after prize. Crowds gathered around, news-
papers told the story, and more and more customers
arrived to buy. Now Mrs. Roberts has several large
greenhouses and more business than she can handle.
What does Mr. Roberts think of it all? He beams with
pride at his wife's accomplishment, and while his work
keeps him busy too, he is intensely interested in the
mechanics of greenhouse operation and helps out in his
spare time.

Then there is the Pennsylvania surgeon who liked
plants. About twelve years ago, Dr. Roland Bachman,
built a 5-foot lean-to greenhouse next to his house. Among
other plants, he acquired two orchids that particularly
took his fancy. Before long, he bought more, propagated
them and soon specialized in them exclusively. An additional greenhouse was built, and because there were
more plants than he could take care of, a professional
grower was hired. Still more plants were started and
more greenhouses built. Now Dr. Bachman has five
greenhouses, fifteen thousand producing plants, and many
progeny coming. Flowers are shipped wholesale to the
Allentown and Philadelphia market—a large operation.

Sometimes husband and wife are equally attracted to
gardening. Mr. and Mrs. Fred Theilemann of New York
started in business three years ago, with a 13- by 26-foot
greenhouse. Fred is an engineer, looking forward to his

time of retirement. In the meantime, husband and wife take care of the greenhouse as a team—a combination that is hard to beat in any business. People come from miles around to buy the potted plants they raise by the thousands. Last year, out of greenhouse income, they put up a second greenhouse, the same type as the first—a sound investment in future security and happiness.

Of course, with most people, this supplementary greenhouse business does not reach such proportions. Some merely buy plants in 2-inch pots or bands and grow them on to sell at maturity. Any number of things can be handled this way—geraniums, cyclamen, cineraria, philodendron, and all the foliage plants.

Others operate their greenhouses after the first of the year to raise bedding plants for spring sales which are so popular in rural and suburban areas. If desired, garden supplies can be sold, too, along with fruits and vegetables in season.

Still other gardeners enjoy using the home greenhouse for a small retail florist business. They buy most of the flowers they make up and sell for weddings, parties, and funerals. Much of the work can be done in the home while the greenhouse becomes a show house—an attention-getter and storage place for ferns, and other plants that are rented or sold. Before taking on such a business, however, it is well to seek experience by working for a florist, or you can take a course at a florists' school.

If you just want to earn enough to pay for your greenhouse and fuel, that is easy, too. For in every neighborhood, there is a demand for house plants in variety as well as corsages of camellias, orchids, carnations, or whatever you have on hand. But no matter what form your greenhouse business takes, vocations are few and far between that can offer so much in health and recreation.

23. Calendar for Greenhouse Planting

Cool Greenhouse 45° to 50°

NAME	PLANT SEEDS, BULBS OR CUTTINGS	DATE TO BENCH OR POT	SPECIAL REQUIREMENTS	TIME OF BLOOM
Agathea	Jan.	July		Dec. through May
Agapanthus	Root stock in Aug.	Aug.	Water moderately in fall and midwinter	April or later
Ageratum	Cuttings—Aug.	Sept.	Very susceptible to white fly	Feb. through late spring
Alyssum	Aug. to Sept.	Aug. to Sept.	Excellent border for bench	Dec. through spring
Anemone	Sept.	Sept.	Buy well-cured bulbs	Jan. through Mar.
Aster	Dec. through April	Feb. through June	Responds to artificial light	Apr. through July
Begonia—tuberous wax	Feb.—pot bulbs Seeds, cuttings any time	Feb.	Partial shade in summer Best raised from seed	Aug. through Oct. Year round
Boston Yellow Daisy	Cuttings—July through Aug.	Nov.	Responds to artificial light	Feb. 15 on
Bouvardia	Cuttings—Feb.	March	Pinch Sept. 1	Dec. through Jan.
Browallia	Seeds—July through Aug.	Pot Sept. through Oct.	Excellent for hanging baskets	Jan. on
Calceolaria	July to Aug.	Pot Oct.	Keep water off foliage	May through June
Calendula	July to Dec.	Sept. through Feb.	40° to 45°	Nov. through May

Candytuft	Dec.—Clumps	Late Jan.	Keep on dry side	May through June
Canterbury Bells	Spring	Clumps after Dec. 15	After freezing	May
Carnation	Cuttings—Dec. to Mar.	May through Aug.	Carry in garden through summer	Late Nov.
Centaurea Cyanus	Dec.	Feb.	Responds to artificial light	April on
Chrysanthemums Early Midseason Late	April to May May May	May June June to July	Darken for earlier blooms	Sept. through Oct. Oct. through Jan. Dec. through Feb.
Chrysanthemums Annual	Oct. through Jan.	Dec. through Feb.	Artificial light for earlier blooms	Apr. through July
Cineraria	May through Aug.	Pot—June to Sept.		Christmas on
Clarkia	Dec.	Late Jan.	Keep on dry side	May
Cyclamen	In cool cellar—July and Aug.	Sept. to Nov.		18 months— Nov. through April
Daphne	Plants from coldframes	Feb. 1		Apr. through May
Didiscus	Aug.	Oct.		Feb. through April
Feverfew	Oct. through Dec.	Feb.	Responds to artificial light	May through June
Forget-me-not	Aug. to Sept.	Sept. to Oct.	Keep water off foliage	Jan. through spring
Freesia	Aug. through Sept.	Aug. through Sept.		Dec. through Feb.
Genista	Cuttings—Aug.	Sept. through Oct.	45° to 50°	Mar. through April

CALENDAR FOR GREENHOUSE PLANTING—Continued
Cool Greenhouse 45° to 50°—Continued

NAME	PLANT SEEDS, BULBS OR CUTTINGS	DATE TO BENCH OR POT	SPECIAL REQUIREMENTS	TIME OF BLOOM
Geranium	Cuttings—Sept.	Sept. through Oct.	45° to 50°	May on
Baby Gladiolus	Dec. through Feb.	Dec. through Feb.		May through June
Gladiolus tristis con-color	Corms—Nov.	Nov.	50° After flowering, set out in garden	Feb. to late spring
G. blandus	Corms—Nov.	Nov.	Dry off after flowering	Feb. to Mar.
Godetia	Dec.	Flat in late Jan.	Keep on dry side	June
Gypsophila Annual	Sept.	Oct.	Artificial light	Dec. on
Lachenalia	Bulbs—Aug. to Sept. Set in coldframe until Nov. or Dec.	Aug. to Sept.	50° Avoid drafts. Store dry until August.	Jan. and Feb.
Larkspur	Nov.	Jan.	50° to 55°	Mar. through June
Marguerite	Cuttings—March	Aug. through Nov.	50° to 55°	Dec. through Jan.
Marigold	Aug. 1 to Sept. 1	Sept. 15 to Oct. 15	Winter-flowering 50° to 55°	Nov. through Jan.
Nasturtium	Aug. to Sept.	Oct.	Grow in pot or bench	Dec. through June
Nemesia	Dec.	Flat late in Jan.	Keep on dry side	May through June
Nerine	Bulbs—May to June	May to June	50° A complete drying-off period is essential.	Sept. to Nov.

	July through Aug.	Nov.	Artificial light	Dec. through Mar.
Pansy				Dec. through Mar.
Primula— Sinensis Obconica Malacoides	Mar. through April Aug. May	Pot May Pot Oct. Pot July		April on Mar. and later Jan. and later
Ranunculus	Sept. to Oct.	Oct.		Feb. on
Salpiglossis	Dec.	Feb.		May through June
Schizanthus	Aug. to Sept.	Oct. to Nov.	Pinch twice before mid Oct.	Mar. through April
Snapdragon	Jan. July through Nov.	March Aug. through Nov.		April through June Nov. through May
Stevia	Cuttings—Mar. through May	Sept.		Dec. through Feb.
Stock	Nov. through Feb. Aug. through Sept.	Jan. through April Sept. through Oct.		April through June Christmas through Feb.
Sweet Pea	Jan. through Feb. June Aug. through Nov.	Jan. through Feb. June Aug. through Nov.		April through June Sept. through Dec. Nov. through May
Tulbaghia	Offsets—any season	Any season	45° Give plenty of water when making growth.	Intermittently
Veltheimia viridifolia	Bulbs—Nov. or Dec.	Nov. or Dec.	50° After blooming grow in full sun and dry off completely.	Early or late spring
Wedgwood Iris	Late Oct.	Late Oct.		Jan. through Feb.

CALENDAR FOR GREENHOUSE PLANTING
Moderate to Warm Greenhouse 55° to 70°

NAME	PLANT SEEDS, BULBS OR CUTTINGS	DATE TO BENCH OR POT	SPECIAL REQUIREMENTS	TIME OF BLOOM
Amaryllis	September to Dec.	Oct. to Jan.	60°—Dry off in Aug.	Feb. to March
Azalea	Pot when received	Sept. to Jan.	Cool until Jan. Then 60°	Dec. and later
Asparagus plumosus or Sprengeri	Divisions—May	May	50° to 60°	
Astilbe	Clumps—after frost	Nov. and later	55° to 60°	90 days
Begonia—wax	Jan. through Feb.	Pot in April	55°	Aug. on
Begonia—Christmas Marjorie Gibbs Melior	Cuttings—Nov.	12 months later	55° to 60°	90 days
Boston Fern	Runners in July		60°	12 or more months
Bougainvillea	Cuttings—Mar. to April	Pot—May to June	Cool until Mar. then 60°	April through May
Calla, Yellow	Flat—peat moss, high temp. Sept. through Dec.	November	Pot after 2 wks. 60°	Mar. through April
Calla, White		Sept. to Dec.	Pot after 2 wks. 55°	Feb. on
Christmas Cactus	Cuttings—Sept.	October	55° to 60°	Dec. through Feb.
Coleus	Seed—March; Cuttings—Sept.	October	55°	Spring

Clivia miniata	Plants—Feb.	Feb.	60° Water moderately in fall and winter and grow at 45° to 50°	Late winter and spring
Crinum	Bulbs—Nov. to Dec.	Dec.	55° to 65° Acid soil and good drainage is essential.	April to summer
Daffodils	Pot or Flats—Oct. to Nov.	Jan. through Feb.	Store 40° to 50° until Jan.	4 to 6 wks.
Gardenia	Cuttings—Nov. through Dec.	Sept.	60° to 65°	Christmas on
Geranium	Cuttings—Aug. through Sept.	Aug. through Oct.	55° Pinch until Feb. 15	March on
Gerberia	Seeds—Feb. through Mar. Divisions June	Aug. through Sept.	55° to 60° Outside summer	Dec. on
Gloriosa Rothschildiana	Tubers—Dec. or Jan.	Dec. or Jan.	60° Store tubers dry until fall.	March
Cloxinia	Tubers—Jan. through Feb. Seeds in March.	Jan., Feb. and Mar.	60°	June-Aug. Aug.-Sept.
Haemanthus coccineus multiflorus Katharinae	Bulbs— Feb. to May Feb. to May Feb. to May	Feb. to May Feb. to May When received	50° to 60° Rest in summer Rest in winter Evergreen, do not dry off.	Fall Summer to fall Spring or Summer

CALENDAR FOR GREENHOUSE PLANTING—*Continued*
Moderate to Warm Greenhouse 55° to 70°—Continued

NAME	PLANT SEEDS, BULBS OR CUTTINGS	DATE TO BENCH OR POT	SPECIAL REQUIREMENTS	TIME OF BLOOM
Hydrangea	Coldframes—until Jan.	January	50° to 70°	April through May
Hyacinth	Pot—Oct. to Nov.	Jan. through Feb.	Store 35° until Jan. Then 55° to 60°	3 to 5 wks.
Kalanchoe	Seed—Jan.	Aug. and Sept.	60° Darken	Dec.
Lantana	Cuttings—Aug. on	Sept. on	60°	May on
Lilium—				
speciosum album	8-9 cm. bulbs—Aug.		55°	Jan.
auratum	Pot singly. 8-9 cm. bulbs	May	55° to 60°	Jan.
candidium	Pot—Aug. through Sept.	Mar. 15 to 30	45° to 60° until Mar. Then 55°	May
erabu	Pot—Nov. through Dec.	Nov. through Dec.	60° to 70°	Feb. through April
formosum		Sept.	55° to 60°	Jan.
regal	Pot 18 cm. bulbs—Jan.	April through Dec.	55° to 60°	Mar. through April
speciosum rubrum	Pot—April through Dec.	Feb. through Mar.	55°	Sept. through June
tenuifolium	Pot—Oct.		Coldframe Feb. through Mar. Then 55°	8 weeks
tigrinum	Pot—June through July	June through July	50° to 70°	Oct. through Nov.
Ornithogalum	Bulbs—Aug.	Oct.	55° to 65° After flowering let bulbs dry off gradually.	Midwinter
Philodendron	Cuttings—Oct.	Nov. 1	55° to 60°	

Poinsettias	Cuttings—June to Aug.	Sept. through Oct.	60° to 65°	Christmas on
Roses in pots	Pot when received	Jan.	Cool until Jan. Then 55° to 60°	12 weeks
Saintpaulia	Cuttings—Dec. through Apr.	Feb. through June	70°	almost constant
Tulips Single Early	Pot—Oct. to Nov.	Jan. through Feb.	Store 35° to 40° until Jan. Then 55° to 60°	4 weeks
Double Early	Pot—Oct. to Nov.	Jan. through Feb.	Store 35° to 40° until Jan. Then 55° to 60°	4 weeks
Breeder Tulips	Pot—Oct. to Nov.	Feb.	50° to 70°	4 to 6 wks.
Darwin	Pot—Oct. to Nov.	Jan. through Feb.	Store 35° to 40° until Jan. Then 55° to 60°	4 to 6 wks.
Vallota	Bulbs—Nov. to Dec.	When received	50° to 55° Perfect drainage is essential.	Spring or summer

NOTE: The dates in the calendar give the span of time during which seeds, bulbs, and cuttings are planted, and the span during which they bloom. Since plants make growth faster during some periods of the year than others, the length of time for maturity varies. For instance, snapdragons planted in July will, under good conditions, bloom in late November or early December, while those planted in November will start to bloom in March or April.

Index